Communication and Society

General Editor: James Curran

SEEING AND BELIEVING

The influence of television

Greg Philo

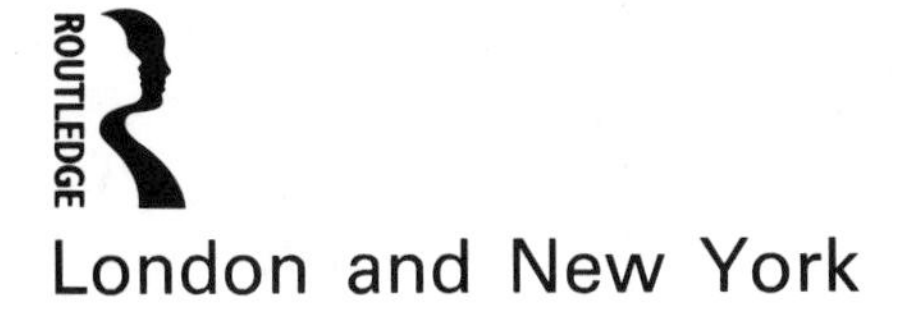

London and New York

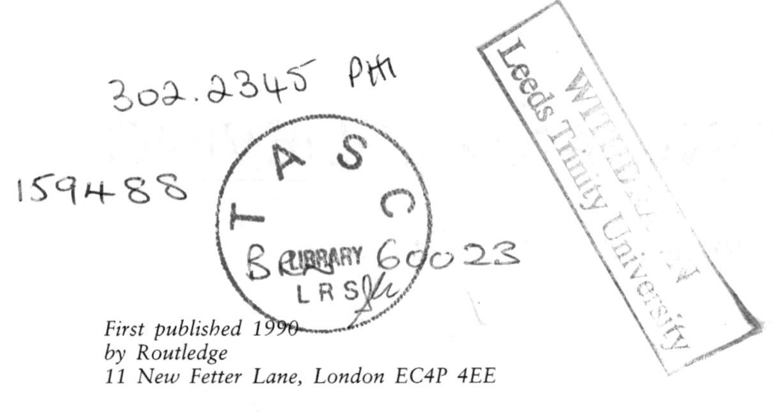

First published 1990
by Routledge
11 New Fetter Lane, London EC4P 4EE

Simultaneously published in the USA and Canada
by Routledge
a division of Routledge, Chapman and Hall, Inc.
29 West 35th Street, New York, NY 10001

Phototypeset by Input Typesetting Ltd, London

Printed in Great Britain by Biddles Ltd, Surrey

British Library Cataloguing in Publication Data

Philo, Greg
Seeing and believing: the influence of television, Greg Philo – (Communication and society)
1. Great Britain. Society. Role of Television
I. Title II. Series
302.2'345
ISBN 0–415–03620–8 ISBN 0–415–03621–6 (pbk.)

Library of Congress Cataloging in Publication Data

Philo, Greg
Seeing and believing: the influence of television/Greg Philo.
p. cm.
Includes bibliographical references.
ISBN 0–415–03620–8 – ISBN 0–415–03621–6 (pbk.)
1. Television broadcasting – Influence. I. Title.
PN1992.6.P55 1990 *89–10904*
302.23'45–dc20

Contents

Illustrations

Acknowledgements

Thanks first of all to Rene and Dick Philo who have constantly helped and encouraged and without whom this work would not have taken place. Thanks also to May, Sarah-May, and John-Mark Philo for putting up with the stress of it going on. Great thanks are also due to the members of the Glasgow University Media Group who have helped me, especially John Eldridge, David Miller, Peter Beharrell, John Hewitt, and Kevin Williams, for their constructive comments and criticisms. Thanks also to James Curran for his very helpful comments and suggestions, to Eve and Marilyn Maine for study facilities, and to Cathy Irvine and Tricia McAveney. For inspiration and good advice, thanks to James Menzies, Edward, Marilyn, Jason, and Christopher Hall and Jim, Mary, Stephen, Emma, and Ross Menzies. There are many others who helped. Thanks to Kathleen Davidson for her great skills in audio typing and in preparing the manuscript. Thanks to Colin Reid for his general skills and also to Trevor Graham and Parlane MacFarlane for photography. Thanks also to John Underwood, Sue Inglish, Huw Beynon, Kay Sillars, Frank Mosson, and Michael Crick. Many people also helped in setting up the research study in different parts of the country. Thanks to Steve and Lynne Colton, Henry and Jane Ball, Kate Phillips, Alec Murray, and Donald Fletcher of the STUC. Thanks also to Helen Bulaitis, Elaine Smith, Sally Stevenson, Ian Turner, Graham Crompton, and Mike Retham, and to Les and Dave Hammond, Margaret and Keith Bradley, Richard Philo, and Fred and Irene Shedden. Thanks again to all these people for going to so much time and trouble and for helping with such good grace.

‘The thing that most of all comes to mind about what was shown on TV was that they were trying to drive us back to work.’

Yorkshire miner

‘At one time, of course, Mr MacGregor was knocked over by this rabble.’

Beckenham resident

‘Seeing is believing.’

Glasgow resident

Introduction

Television is the main source of information on national and world events for most of us. But do we believe what we see and what we are told? It has always been difficult to show how media *content* relates to public *belief*.

It is possible sometimes to make broad assertions about the 'effects' of the media. One way of doing this is to compare the results of opinion polls with media content. For example, research into media coverage of the disease AIDS has shown correlations between themes developed in the media and changes in public knowledge. In 1987 the Media Group at Glasgow University analysed television and press coverage of AIDS for the DHSS and the Central Office of Information, as part of a wider study of public belief in this area (COI, 1988). Table 0.1 shows the number of references in the media to various ways of catching AIDS. Table 0.2 shows the percentage of a population sample who showed an awareness of these without being prompted.

These tables show how trends in public awareness can relate

Table 0.1 *Ways AIDS 'can be caught'*
(*Number of references press and television March/April 1986*)

Sexual contact	85
Blood	27
Saliva/Kissing	20
Injections/Injecting drugs	172

Table 0.2 *Main ways of catching AIDS (spontaneous responses)*
(British Market Research Bureau)

Sexual contact	86%
Blood	63% falling
Saliva/Kissing	24% falling
Injections/Injecting drugs	22% rising

to media content. For example, there is a constant flow of references in the media to sexual contact as a way of catching AIDS. Public awareness of this is high and steady at 86%. But in the media, blood and saliva/kissing are both low at 27 and 20 references. The BMRB opinion study shows that these are both falling in people's awareness (relative to earlier studies). The dominant theme in media reports on ways of catching AIDS at this time was injections/injecting drugs, with a total of 172 references. This is the only category of public awareness that is shown to be rising.

Such studies can indicate general trends, but they are still couched at a very broad level. They show little of how any specific section of the public relates to information from the media or the processes by which beliefs develop.

There is a long history in communication research of attempting to explain these key relationships.

From 'mass society' to 'reinforcement'

Some of the earliest attempts to explain the relation between the media and public belief used the concept of the mass society. This offered a view of the contemporary world as composed of fragmented individuals, increasingly subject to powerful propaganda messages. Its influence on media theory grew in part from the historical experience of the rise of fascism in Europe and from how totalitarian political systems were understood to have used the control of communications. The theory of the mass society has its roots in nineteenth-century sociology with its focus on the breakdown of organic traditional societies and the emergence of large scale urban society. Leon Bramson (1961), in a study of the influence of the theory, traces its view of the isolated individual through the work of theorists such as H. Marcuse and T. Adorno of the Frankfurt school. C. Wright Mills (1959 and 1963) also utilizes the concept, although he did not believe that contemporary public opinion in the USA was wholly controlled by the media. He does, however, write of a growing problem in which:

> in the mass society of media markets, competition goes on between the crowd of manipulators with their mass media on the one hand, and the people receiving their communications

> on the other. 'Answering back' by the people is systematically unavailable.
>
> (1963, p. 577, quoted in Eldridge, 1987)

The theoretical arguments on the mass society had some features in common with behaviourist trends in social science which saw the individual as 'responding' to direct stimuli.

Beliefs about the impact of media had also been strengthened by key instances of its effects. These included the notorious rendering of *War of the Worlds* by Orson Welles in 1938, which panicked New Yorkers (Cantril, H., *et al.*, 1940), and the effects of Kate Smith's appeals for American war bonds (raising 39 million dollars in one day), which was the subject of a study by Robert Merton (1946). The search for such direct media effects on individual behaviour was extended in the post-war period to the study of areas such as television violence and the effect of exposure to election coverage on voting behaviour. But the relation between media messages, belief and behaviour was found to be more complex than a simple stimulus followed by a response. In practice it was very difficult to show that exposure to a set of violent images produced measurable effects on children's behaviour. The reliability of the experimental methods used in this area was questioned and the results were inconclusive.[1]

Dennis McQuail (1977) writes of a second phase in mass communications research in which the general conclusion was that the media were unlikely to be major contributors to the direct change of individual opinions, attitudes or behaviour. As summarized by Klapper (1960) this view was that:

1 Mass communication ordinarily does not serve as a necessary and sufficient cause of audience effects, but rather functions among and through a nexus of mediating factors and influences.

2 These mediating factors are such that they typically render mass communication a contributory agent, but not the sole cause, in a process of reinforcing the existing conditions. (Regardless of the condition in question – be it the vote intentions of audience members, their tendency toward or away from delinquent behaviour, or their general orientation toward life and its problems – and regardless of

> whether the effect in question be social or individual, the media are more likely to reinforce than to change).
>
> (1960, p. 8)

This signalled a major transformation from seeing the media as an all-powerful force on the individual. The new focus was on how messages were received and used by people in the audience either as individuals or in the context of small social groups.[2] The 'uses and gratifications' approach assumed that the individuals' values and interests led to a selective perception and shaping of what was seen and heard. What was taken from the media might depend upon individual preferences and psychology. For example, a programme might be attractive to one person for its dramatic or exciting qualities while someone else might be interested in it for the information which it contains. The early research in the USA used survey techniques to ask people about the 'gratifications' which they took from programmes such as quiz shows.[3]

The attempts which had been made to gauge media effects had largely focused on possible changes in attitude following exposure to campaigns on issues such as health, voting or buying goods. The general conclusion was that they had no or very little effect.[4] But, as McQuail argues, the results were in part conditioned by the limited nature of the studies:

> These were mainly experiments or surveys designed to measure short-term changes occurring in individuals, and concentrating especially on the key concept of attitude. Alternative research approaches might take a longer time span, pay more attention to people in their social context, look at what people know (in the widest sense) rather than at their attitudes and opinions, take account of the uses and motives of the audience member as mediating any effect, look at structures of belief and opinion and social behaviour rather than individual cases, take more notice of the *content* whose effects are being studied.
>
> (1977, p. 74)

As he notes, there was often a failure to examine the specific content of messages and their meaning to the audience in terms of how they related to wider systems of social values and beliefs.[5] The media are part of a process of cultural reproduction and their content consists of much more than isolated pieces of information or opinion. Thus a campaign message during an election does not simply tell us how to vote. It also implicitly assumes the legitimacy of a certain type of political system. Similarly, an advertisement for a product may contain implicit assumptions about 'acceptable' or desirable lifestyles. McQuail's point is that the search for instant, measurable effects on the individual has led to a neglect of the role of the media in developing political and social cultures over long periods of time:

> the media work most directly on consciousness by providing the constructed images of the world and of social life and the definitions of social reality. In effect, the audience member learns about his or her social world and about himself from the media presentation of society (given that most of the time, most of this is not directly accessible). The media provide the materials for responding to experience and these accumulate over time in a long-term process of socialisation. The effects of the media on the individual are not only indirect, they may have happened long ago, certainly in the past.
>
> (1977, p. 76)

The media are conveying much more than a single message on who to vote for, or which brand of product to buy. Messages are situated within political and cultural assumptions about what is normal and acceptable within the society. In news production, these include beliefs about hierarchies of access, about who has the right to speak, what are the key political institutions, and what is 'acceptable' behaviour.[6] On an everyday level, the television, press, and radio also provide information about specific events, which tacitly relate to these unspoken assumptions. For example, news journalists might assume a consensus amongst their audience that violence should not be used in resolving political/industrial disputes. News reports might then give specific instances of violent behaviour (as in the miners' strike), and allocate blame to one 'side' in the conflict. In doing so the reports assume a consensus on the value that violence is 'wrong'. The reports are thus situated within, and contribute to, political and social cultures which are constantly developing.

In this way the news may offer a 'preferred' view of events, but we cannot assume that its audience will all accept this interpretation. The consensus that violence is wrong is not likely to be matched by a common agreement on who should be blamed. For example, attitudes on whether police or pickets are more likely to start trouble may vary between different groups in the society (as between groups of working-class trade unionists and middle-class professionals). Such differences within the audience may affect the way in which information from the media is received. This acceptance or rejection of the television message is conditioned partly by differences in political culture. Such cultures are not static and cannot be seen as simply determining how individuals respond. The cultures themselves are clearly subject to change from a variety of influences, one of which could be new information which is received from the media. One of the findings of this study is that political cultures do not always insulate those within them from the preferred media view. Trade unionists and others who were sympathetic to the striking miners were more likely to reject the news account of the origins of violence, but they did not always do so.

Some new approaches

The uses and gratifications perspective offered a relatively static model, in which individuals were seen as using specific messages according to their own interests and purposes. If there was an effect on belief it was largely construed as being one of reinforcement. But as we have seen, this model does not come to terms with the complexity either of what is being transmitted by the media or of the cultures within which the messages are being received.

A contemporary variant on this perspective is the argument that what people see and understand in media messages depends upon their pre-existing beliefs or political 'bias'. This theory has appeared most recently in work by Michael Tracey and Guy Cumberbatch who pursued the general theme that 'bias lies in the eye of the beholder' (Cumberbatch, 1986; Tracey, 1986).

There are difficulties with this perspective. We can accept that what people understand and believe is not simply a result of what they are told by the media. But there are problems with the assertion that our understanding of new information is determined by pre-existing cultural and political assumptions. The most obvious questions are: where do frameworks of belief come from?, how do they develop over time?, and how may they alter in relation to new information and new experiences? We cannot write off the effect of the media simply because a small number of stimuli are not seen to have much effect on developed systems of belief.

If we are to understand the role of the media in the reproduction or development of these systems, then a detailed analysis of media content is an initial priority. In pursuing this, a number of theorists have recently examined the processes by which news reporting can establish both the priorities of discussion and the ways in which controversial issues are to be understood.[7] These 'ways of understanding' or interpretative frameworks were seen as being related to class perspectives in the society as a whole. It was also assumed that if the content of news was produced from within such perspectives then it might be interpreted differently according to the class position and cultural assumptions of different groups within the audience.[8]

The communication process does not, therefore, consist of the media providing stimuli to isolated individuals who interpret them according to fixed preconceptions. Rather, the cultures of any given moment are part of a social *process* in which beliefs are produced and contested in the conflict between groups and classes. The media are one site of this struggle to establish the dominance of some ways of understanding. This is so whether the arguments relate to economic or political policy, such as on the role of strikes in the decline of the economy, or whether they are about definitions of political action such as whether a 'terrorist' is to be called a 'guerilla' or a 'freedom fighter'. No one claims that exposure to a preferred media view will necessarily and instantly transform political allegiance. But it is crucial to study the manner in which such arguments are developed in media accounts and in audience beliefs to form strands of political cultures, and to analyse the processes by which they are overlaid by new information and different forms of experience.

To examine these processes requires a methodology which focuses on groups rather than individuals and which can reveal how what is understood from the media relates to existing systems of belief. In pursuing this it did not seem very useful to show audiences a particular programme and then attempt to gauge possible 'effects'. Instead it seemed more fruitful to ask groups to write their own programmes. This would show what they thought the content of the news to be on a given issue. It might then be possible to compare this with what they actually believed to be true and to examine why they either accepted or rejected the media account. This approach made members of the public temporarily into journalists and became the basis for this study.

The current work

As a whole, this book has been organized such that the introduction deals broadly with the main problems in studying communications and audiences as they were understood up until the 1970s. At this point there were major new developments in critical theory and specifically in the analysis of media content and its reception. In Europe and the USA there was an intensification of interest in the ability of the media to influence public consciousness. The concept of 'agenda setting' was used to indicate the ability of the media to establish the priorities for public discussion. In other words, the media could tell the public what to think *about* if not exactly what to think. Rogers and Dearing (1988) describe the rise of this new paradigm in the United States:

> The new communication scholars typically had predoctoral experience in journalism or broadcasting, followed by social science training emphasizing the work of Lewin, Hovland, Lasswell, and Lazarsfeld, plus courses in statistical methods and quantitative research methods. The new breed 'knew' from their personal backgrounds that the mass media had effects, even though the scientific findings of the field's four founders generally indicated only minimal effects of the media. This paradox between past professional beliefs versus scientific results sent the new communication scholars off in search of evidence of strong media effects.
>
> (1988, p. 565)

In Britain, there were attempts to go beyond this paradigm by analysing the 'preferred meaning' of news accounts and the manner in which television and press reporting was organized around specific ways of understanding (Hall, 1970; Philo, Beharrell, and Hewitt, 1977; Glasgow University Media Group, 1976, 1980). The main body of the research in this volume is a contribution towards these new approaches and follows from the work on news content which was initially undertaken by the Glasgow University Media Group. The last chapter relates the new findings on both content and reception to the most contemporary debates in this area.

1

Making the news

Methodology and sample

The procedure for this study grew from a series of pilot investigations with students at Glasgow University. Initially these were with groups of about five people. They were asked to imagine that they were journalists writing a short news item on the 1984/5 miners' strike and were given a series of photographs which had been taken directly from the television screen. The photos were all from news programmes during the summer of 1984 and were selected to represent the main themes in coverage of the strike. These were 'negotiations', 'meetings', 'statements by leaders', 'picketing', 'police', 'mining communities/support groups', and 'the return to work'.[1] In practice the pictures could be used to illustrate many different themes. My interest was in seeing how people would select pictures to illustrate their stories and it was left open as to which ones they could choose. It was also suggested to the groups that they might write different types of news programmes. For example, they might be ITN, BBC, or an American News or even an 'access' programme made by either the trade unions or by a right-wing pressure group.

These early pilots were conducted from November 1984 to February 1985, while the strike was actually in progress. The strike had begun in March 1984 and ended one year later in March 1985.

In the stories that the students wrote at this time, one picture began to recur in a very notable way. It was of a shot-gun lying on a table (Picture 1). The actual news story which it was from concerned a miner, who was breaking the strike. He stated on the news that he was prepared to use the gun to defend himself. But it was apparent that in the imaginary news stories that were being written, the gun was persistently being put into the hands of *striking* miners. This was done even by students who were clearly sympathetic to the miners' cause. In the year following the end of the strike several more groups of students repeated the exercise and the familiar pattern recurred of the gun being placed with the strikers/pickets. Here is an example from a group eight months after the strike had ended:

> *Newscaster:* Good evening. Early this morning trouble flared at Orgreave Colliery. Police tried to make way for working miners, but during scuffles with pickets, came under violent attack as missiles were thrown . . . Several horses were lamed by sharp metal objects which were strewn on the road. Police later displayed objects confiscated including a shot-gun.
>
> (November 1985)

The gun was not always included in such violent circumstances. In this example a group of students produced a 'trade union access programme'. This was written in January 1985 while the strike was still in progress.

> A picket was arrested today on gun charges. He was arrested near a picket line and taken to the local police station although he was later released with no charges being made. He was out shooting rabbits with his double-barrelled 12-bore to supplement food at the local miners' institute, where a food kitchen has been set up by a 'women's support group'. Mr Smith was shooting on land where he had permission from the local farmer; and when arrested he had the gun in his case, and the cartridges safely in a secure holder.

On one occasion the ownership of the gun was left indeterminate by students who were again writing a 'trade union access programme':

> It was later revealed by representatives of the union that this shot-gun had been found on the scene of the demonstration. A union representative exclusively revealed this picture of the gun which was taken from the scene into the security of his home in order to prevent any unsubstantiated claims by the police that this weapon was used by a miner.
>
> (December 1985)

Since this was the only occasion in the student groups where the ownership of the gun was not specified, I asked this group how they had arrived at the content of their programme. They said that on seeing the picture of the gun they had assumed that in reality it had belonged to a striking miner. But because they were writing a trade union piece they had then 'consciously slanted the news away from it'.

In the year after the strike, the exercise began to take on a more defined shape. It was then conducted on a more formal basis with a clearly sampled range of social groups and a set of questions which could be answered about beliefs and information sources.[2]

The exercise

This phase began one year after the strike ended. Each group was given a set of twelve pictures (pictures 1–12) and asked, as with the students, to write an imaginary news story. They were now specifically told to include the picture of the shot-gun. In the event, I worked with an average number of nine people at a time who were then subdivided into smaller groups.

They were asked to write a 'normal' BBC news but it was also suggested that they could, if they wished, write a trade union 'access' programme.[3] In practice, this worked as a way of filtering people who were sympathetic to the miners into a single group. The purpose was to see if such a group would still give the gun to the strikers.

The normal procedure was for the news story to be written first. In practice these were completed very quickly, usually within ten to fifteen minutes. The series of questions were then read out, to which people wrote individual answers. This was followed by individual interviews to clarify points which had been made in written replies. These clarifications were also written down by the group members on their answer sheets. At the end of a session a spontaneous discussion would sometimes develop amongst the group and I would be asked about the study and the results of it up to that point. This was not curtailed as it was important to make the whole thing as open-ended as possible while ensuring that all of the groups completed the news writing exercise and answered the same basic questions. It was essential to include both the exercise and the questions as seperate elements of the method. This is because the writing of the story could operate either as a projective test (i.e. reproducing the beliefs of group members about events in the strike) or as a re-enactment test (i.e. representing what they believed the

Illustrations 1–12: Pictures given to the groups

1

2

3

4

5

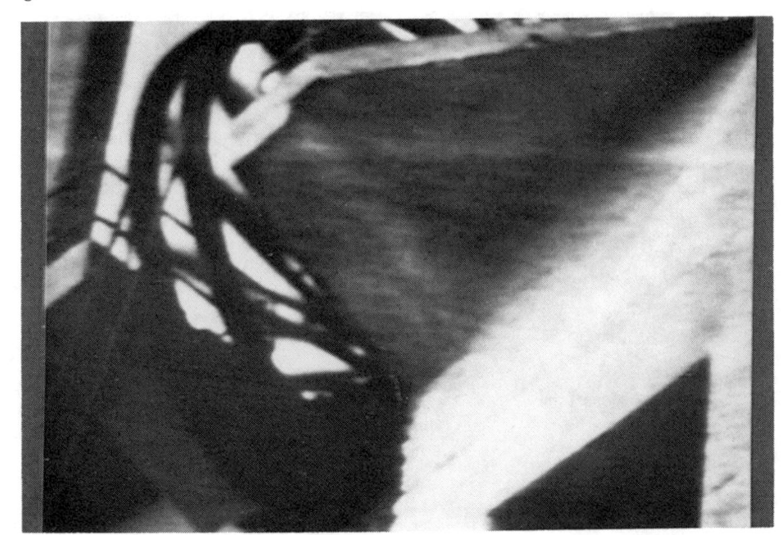

6

7

8

9

10

11

12

television account would be). The questions were necessary to clarify this and to reveal individual beliefs on issues such as the ownership of the gun.

The questions

These were put to each group immediately after completion of the news-writing exercise.

Question 1 *When you first saw the picture of the gun, who did you think it belonged to?*

In practice the picture of the gun led to intense argument within the groups as to how it should be included. The purpose of the question was to identify how each person thought of the weapon. For example, did they think of it as being used in interpersonal violence, or as having a more functional use, such as shooting rabbits for soup kitchens? It was also important to know whether the gun was associated with one 'side' in the dispute or whether the ownership was left indeterminate.

Studies of television news content suggest that violence was very largely linked with the striking miners. An analysis by Alastair Hetherington (1985) showed that violence outside collieries was attributed over ten times as much on the news to miners/pickets as to the police (p. 275).

In the event, beliefs about the gun gave some insight into how different groups within the television audience understood the origins of violence within the strike.

Question 2 *Does the BBC news have a point of view? Does it, for example, favour one political party over another, or it is neutral? Is it biased, unbiased, pro-establishment, anti-establishment, accurate, impartial? How would you describe it?*

Question 3 *Does ITN operate from a point of view? Do you think it is the same as BBC news or is it different in some way?*

It was important to know if group members had strong views on whether the news organisations were thought to be neutral. Such views might affect how the groups' own 'news programmes' were produced. For example, a group believing that the BBC was 'pro-establishment' might produce a tongue-in-cheek version which did not match their own beliefs about what had actually occurred in the strike. In the event, attitudes to the BBC (rather than ITN) proved to be important for this study – because the groups were writing 'BBC' programmes and because of the recent controversy which has surrounded the BBC's news coverage following the criticisms made of it by Conservative politicians.

A note on method: question 2 is asked in this lengthy way in order to keep a range of options open in the mind of the person answering. It seemed important not to point the question in a particular direction by asking, for example, 'Do you think the BBC is biased?'

Question 4 In the miners' strike, did you think that the picketing that took place was mostly violent or mostly peaceful?[4]

Question 5 Was the picketing that you saw on the television news mostly violent or mostly peaceful?

Question 6 What was the source of your information for question 4; what made you think the picketing was either violent or peaceful?

These three questions were central to the study. The academic research on news content by Cumberbatch *et al.* (1986) suggests that over 60 per cent of the coverage of picketing concentrated on picket violence, with only 3 per cent reporting peaceful picketing. If people believed that most of the picketing shown on television news was violent, then did they also believe such images to be a true account of what picket lines were like for most of the time? Equally important, for what reasons might people reject the images as representing what had typically happened?

One source of such a rejection might be the differences in the descriptions of picketing given in various parts of the media. For example the 'quality' press might differ from the television news. The main focus for this study was television since it is the principal information medium for most people. But there may well have been contradictions between what was seen on television and what was read in some newspapers. If so, this should show in answers to question 6 (which in practice it did). It also seemed likely that question 6 would give other clues as to why people might reject what they had seen in the news.

Question 7 Of all the issues that were covered in the strike, what do you think was on television news the most?

The salience of some images might have affected people's perception of what was actually shown. Was it, for example, the violent images that 'stuck' and overwhelmed other memories? Or is it that people simply 'switch off' from some parts of the news and remember what was on very selectively?

To be able to judge this, we need some knowledge of what was actually shown most on television. It is difficult to give an exact answer to this since estimates can vary with how different subjects are categorized. For example, are Miners' Galas, mass demonstrations and mass meetings all the 'same' thing, in which case they would be one large category, or are they all different, in which case they are three smaller ones?

The academic work by Cumberbatch *et al.* (1986) on this came to the conclusion that in terms of issues mentioned on the news 'negotiations' was by far the largest category followed by 'picket-line violence' and 'mining communities'.

Question 8 Of all the things that you saw, what stuck in your own mind the most? If I say the words 'miners' strike' to you what image or event comes most vividly to your mind?

This was an attempt to understand the cultural and political filters which are brought to perception and memory. It was in practice one of the areas which illustrated most clearly the personal beliefs of the group members.

It also seemed likely that there might be a link between answers to this question and the previous one – in the sense that what was meaningful and vivid to the individual might affect the perception of how much had actually been reported on different topics.

Question 9 Which newspaper do you normally read/prefer?

This question was helpful in tracing specific information sources. If a group member wrote simply that their beliefs on picketing were from 'the media' (and meant television news and the press) it was useful to know which paper was read.

As a subsidiary question, the groups were also asked whether their attitude to the police had changed in the period since the miners' strike. It seemed useful to assess whether media coverage had had any effect in this area. It was included following the interviews with police officers in the early stages of the research. Some of them expressed the view that media images of the police were unlikely to have had very dramatic effects on public belief. As we will see, in practice this question was very important in understanding some responses to news reports. There were not usually any direct questions on voting intentions and political allegiances. It seemed likely that some respondents would see such questions as hostile or intrusive and that this might produce a very defensive response. It was important that answers be relatively spontaneous and consequently I relied on the more open-ended approach of allowing people to write freely about their own views and memories in their answer sheets.

The group method

It was important to work with groups rather than to simply interview individuals, as I wished to see how people would work and discuss the issues together. It seemed likely that they would generate ideas more spontaneously with each other than in a structured interview. Such group processes are important since our culture and beliefs are, after all, the product of collective thought and action.[5]

A more practical reason for group work is that these exercises were a very unusual activity for people to undertake. Working in a group minimized the embarrassment of individuals and helped those who found difficulty in writing. In practice there was always one person who would volunteer to be the 'scribe'.

There was a possible problem with this method in that a consensus might be imposed within the group, having the effect of masking individual views. But to some extent those of like minds could go together, by choosing which type of news they wished to do. Additionally, if there was a serious problem of conflicting opinion then in practice the groups subdivided again to produce two different news programmes. The group exercise was in any case followed by the giving of individual answers to the questions.

Selecting the groups

The composition of the groups was also important. The intention was to make them 'natural' in the sense that they had some existence prior to the research project. It seemed less useful to bring together an artificial group composed of individuals selected on criteria such as age, sex, or class. This is not the sort of group in which people usually meet or talk about television programmes.

At the same time, the people did have to be selected such that they could highlight possible differences in perception caused by factors such as class or cultural background. In the event, for the major sample, I interviewed 169 people who fell into four main types.

1 *Groups with a special knowledge or experience of the strike*
These included a group of senior police officers, a group of trade unionists from different unions in Scotland, miners and women's support group members from Yorkshire, and a group of print workers from Fleet Street.
2 *Occupational groups*
These included the staff of a solicitors' office in London and a comparable group in Glasgow; a group of electronics employees in Harlow; and catering staff and supervisors in London Transport.
3 *Special interest groups*
These were groups that came together on a regular basis with a shared common interest. They included mothers' and toddlers' groups in Glasgow, London and Kent, plus a body of elderly people who met as an 'Activity in retirement group' in Glasgow. Because the members of these groups were either retired or had young children, they were mostly not involved in work outside the home.
4 *Residential groups*
These were a series of groups in the south-east of England from Bromley and Beckenham in Kent, and Shenfield in Essex. A table of those who were interviewed is given in Table 1.1.

This selection of groups made it possible to hold constant some key variables such as regional area, while varying others such as class/cultural background. Sometimes these variables could be compared in the same group. Those in the solicitors' offices, for example, encompassed a range of white-collar jobs from secretaries through to the partners of the firms. This made it possible to compare the experiences and beliefs of those working at different occupations within the same building. The whole group could then be compared with another in a similar office but in a different regional area. In the event these variables

Table 1.1 *Groups interviewed*

Group	Number
Groups with special knowledge/experience	
Senior police officers, Cumberland Lodge, Windsor Great Park	8
Trade unionists in Scotland, STUC Education Centre	19
Yorkshire miners/Women's support group	9
Print workers, Fleet Street	9
Occupational groups	
Solicitors' office, Croydon	9
Solicitors' office, Glasgow	18
London Transport catering staff	7
London Transport catering supervisors	6
Electronics staff, Harlow	11
Special interest groups	
Activity in retirement group, Glasgow	14
Women in community centres, Glasgow	10
Mothers' and toddlers' group, Bromley, Kent	9
Penge community playgroup, London	9
Residential groups	
Bromley, Kent	9
Beckenham, Kent	12
Shenfield, Essex	10

produced clear differences in processes of perception and belief amongst the range of groups.

The use of pictures by the groups

The photographs which the groups used were intended as a stimulus to memory and to provide some possible contexts for stories about the strike. The groups were not instructed to indicate which pictures related precisely to the different parts of their stories. This was important since in actual news programmes there is often a very loose relationship between the film that is shown and the news text. Television professionals refer to film used in this way as 'wallpaper'. It seemed quite legitimate for the groups to have the same attitude to the use of their pictures. In practice, the photographs were often used by them to create a moving collage of images which suggested the events of the stories without being very specific. This had an additional advantage in terms of the construction of the stories, since it enabled the groups to introduce themes for which there were no explicit pictures, such as the role of the miners' wives during the strike. I kept a record of where such themes occurred and also of other variations in the use of the pictures – for example where figures for the return to work were used to indicate the number of pits that were operating. However, it will be clear that my main concerns were, firstly with the ability of the groups to reproduce some of the key themes of news accounts in their written stories and secondly to examine the conditions under which the group members either believed or rejected what they had understood from television news.

Hypotheses

When this study was designed, its main focus was on beliefs about the nature and origins of violence in the strike. The test using the picture of the gun was chosen to illustrate how different audiences might link violence to the various 'sides' in the dispute and how assumptions about the ownership of the firearm might vary with different class, cultural, and regional influences.

The method employed in this study was relatively untried and it soon became apparent that the research results were revealing relationships which were unexpected. These included the finding that the groups were able to produce news language and key themes from news reports many months after the strike had ended. There were also interesting results on the relation between direct experience and the interpretation of news accounts. These were not anticipated in the original design, and with hindsight it is possible to see how this project could have been organized differently to highlight them. For example, it would have been possible to ask groups to write about specific issues, such as the causes of the dispute or to ask them to produce a 'typical' news headline. Nonetheless, without specific directions, the groups still produced some remarkable material which is included here with the limitations that I have expressed.

We should also be clear about the more general limits of this study. The groups used are varied and illustrate some processes in the perception and belief of news accounts. But the sample as a whole is not large enough to make precise generalizations about the national population. Also, these findings relate directly to the perception of the miners' strike. We cannot make generalizations about all news programmes from them. However, in the final chapter there is an extended commentary on what light the findings do shed on existing research in this area.

2

Practical experience and knowledge

The police

This group was brought together at a conference on 'The Media and the Police' at Cumberland Lodge, Windsor Great Park, in April 1986. Eight police officers took part in the news-writing exercise. Seven of these worked in a group together and one who came later worked alone. They spanned the ranks of Inspector, Chief Inspector, and Superintendent, and were from a range of police forces including those of South Wales, Greater Manchester, Lincolnshire, Humberside, Northamptonshire, Warwickshire, and the Metropolitan (London) area.

Between them the officers had extensive knowledge of the strike and of police operations within it. In addition most had specific experience of working with the media in the press and public relations offices of their own forces.

Writing the news

The main group of seven officers was subdivided into smaller groups to produce (1) a trade union access-style news, (2) a BBC news, and (3) a news from the point of view of the police. These were as follows:

Trade union news

On a day when in defence of their jobs and livelihood 1,000 't-shirt and trainer' clad mineworkers and their families were the subject of repeated abuse and violent taunts from the ranks of 2,000 paramilitary police of the United Kingdom.

In riot gear so familiar of that of the South American States the police demonstrated their insensitivity and brutality with baton, shield and mounted police against the working classes by charging at them and lashing at will.

The mineworkers were forced to flee in advance of repeated

police charges and it was later claimed by (a senior police officer) of the South Yorkshire police that a loaded shot-gun was found by the police in the wake of the fleeing pickets.

The police stated that they are conducting their own enquiries into the issue.

BBC TV

National Coal Board announced further 13 pits reopened this morning; increased speculation that strike is breaking up; MacGregor's aggressive stance that miners returning.

Scargill rejected claims and stated strike as strong as ever.

Early reports suggest that firearms may be used by miners in the dispute and this gun was recovered from the home of striking miner today. Police state that weapon is unconnected with the dispute although police have confiscated it. They interviewed a man today in connection with a stolen shotgun.

Meanwhile further violence on picket lines during course of day although small number of arrests reported. (A senior police officer) reported that things were much calmer and no further incidents reported. Police officers were able to relax towards the end of the day.

Police news

Today Ian MacGregor Chairman of the National Coal Board announced that the number of miners returning to work continued to increase.

At Bilston Glen, despite massive picketing by striking miners and their families, twelve additional men returned to work today. Extra police were on hand to prevent serious public disorder. During the morning's operation, shots were fired at officers who were engaged in crowd control. One constable received slight injuries. Later a shot-gun was recovered from nearby waste ground. (A senior police officer) said 'This is a serious development in an already sad chapter of industrial relations. I call for calm good sense before somebody is seriously injured or even killed'.

Mr Scargill, President of the National Union of Mineworkers: 'The police are being used as political pawns – I have always feared that someone, somewhere would do something like this.

I call upon the Prime Minister to act and allow my members to return to work by giving us an honourable settlement'.

A further BBC news was produced by a woman police officer who arrived later and worked alone:

BBC news

Today in the miners' strike police officers were fired upon. No officers were injured, but this incident has again heightened tensions and fears for an escalation of violence. One shot was fired and a gun has been recovered. Police have made a number of arrests relating to this incident.

Officers, equipped with shields and helmets, feel they are not protected against such displays of violence and fear for their safety. Officials from the NUM state they have no knowledge of who had fired the gun and deny that it is a member of the NUM.

The 'News' extracts are reproduced here as they were written. Their style varies from staccato phrases (as in a subtitled news) to more natural speech. The group working on the trade union news finished it within a few minutes. They commented that they were able to do this because there was 'only one trade union voice in the strike'. It is instructive that the officers could produce such a clear parody of the 'opposition' case. There is one key difference, however, between their account and that of trade unionists doing the same exercise. The police officers put the gun into a violent context and link it with the pickets. This in fact reflected the views of those who wrote the above story. But not all of the officers presented the gun in this way. The 'BBC' group deliberately avoided associating the gun with the striking miners and said that in their news they were 'putting right rumours in the press about the gun'.

The other two news stories both leave the ownership of the gun indeterminate, but the police are clearly the victims in shootings. In this the sentiments of the writers are quite clear. The author of the last 'BBC news' also made a point about her own values. She was not at the picket lines but her husband was, and she felt an intense personal involvement. This is perhaps reflected in the sentence about 'fear for the safety of officers'. But it is interesting that such a commitment did not colour her own assessment of the amount of 'peace' or 'violence' in picketing. As we shall see, she along with all the others sharply rejected the view that picket lines were generally violent.

The questions – the gun and picketing

The first question was on the ownership of the gun. Two officers replied that they thought it belonged to pickets and three others said that they thought it was being used by striking miners. The remaining three officers would not comment on the ownership until they knew more details, but one did say that he believed the gun came from 'a non-police source'. Their attitude is reflected in the construction of the first 'BBC' news above.

On questions 2 and 3 most of the differences seen between BBC and ITN were stylistic and neither channel was seen as having strong partisan views.

The fourth question on the issue of picketing in the strike was important in that it could potentially highlight any differences between what the officers had seen in the media and their own beliefs based on knowledge and experience of the strike. They were asked 'do you think that picketing during the strike was mostly violent . . . ?' There was literally a chorus of 'No!' They stated that 'a lot of it was good-natured banter'. When the pickets and police did confront each other they described it as being rather like a rugby scrum: 'Come on lads it's time for a good heave' said one officer.

But their most profound memories were of endless frustration as nothing happened at all. They commented on how 'boring' it was 'sitting around in vans' and 'how exhausting the whole business was – one long bad dream'. These were the views of the main group of officers but they were reflected again in the comments of the woman police officer who stated that 'No it was certainly not [mostly violent] – a lot of standing around'.

It is very interesting how closely these descriptions mirror those given later by pickets/miners. Here is a description given by a trade unionist who was picketing in Scotland:

> People would sit around doing very little, police and pickets. Often, police would just sit in their vans until it was nearly time for the shifts to change. Then people would take up their positions and as the working miners went in and out, there

> was a bit of a shove and a bit of a shout and then they would all sit down again for another six hours.

Real-life experiences such as these were seen as being very different from coverage on television news. In answering question 5, all the police officers believed that most of what had been shown was violent. They were also able to name what they saw as odd instances of other types of coverage – such as scenes at Christmas of people sitting around braziers.

Question 6 was superfluous for this group since the source of their knowledge was clear.

Memories and beliefs

Questions 7 and 8 related to the group's beliefs about what had mostly been shown on television news during the strike, and what had made most impact upon them. These questions illustrate how memories can be affected by the salience of some images. More importantly they show how this salience can vary between social groups, i.e., differences in culture and values may condition what is remembered. The answers given by the police officers to question 7 and their comments were as follows:

Question 7 (on news most)

1 Movement of pickets (that's me giving a police answer)
2 Pickets at end of strike/political arguments between Scargill and MacGregor at beginning
3 Arthur Scargill
4 Not know
5 Two sides of argument (negotiations)
6 Negotiations
7 Numbers on strike
8 Pickets

'Negotiations' is not a category of coverage which tends to be very salient in people's minds. But in this case three of the officers gave this and 'arguments' as an answer. This does suggest an exceptional attention to the news. The professional concerns of the police are also shown in their answers to question 8:

Question 8 (most personal impact)

1 Mounted branch officer with truncheon and woman
2 Policeman hitting picket
3 Brick through window of car
4 Repeated taunts of women shouting 'scab, scab' with little children in arms who were also shouting
5 Concrete block on taxi
6 Mounted officers coming back rattling their shields (I remember it because it got a lot of adverse comment)
7 Divisions in family over strike, son not talking to father
8 Woman driving to work – brick going through window [as in 3 above] and soup kitchens, welfare for miners.

In general the answers given here and the writing of the news exercises showed a very detailed knowledge of the strike and media coverage of it. This high level of awareness was echoed in the trade union groups.

Scottish trade unionists

This was a group of nineteen people attending a residential Health and Safety course at the Scottish TUC's education centre. They were from a variety of occupations including white-collar, clerical, and technical as well as firemen, steel, engineering, and construction workers.

The meeting was in April 1986, about fourteen months after the coal dispute had ended.

Writing the news

They were divided into four groups to produce two 'BBC news programmes' and two 'trade union access' programmes. In the event the placing of the shot-gun in the stories created some controversy, reaching a peak in the second trade union group. As a result the group divided itself and produced two different stories. The final stories are as follows:

First trade union news

The National Coal Board reported today that thirteen miners from the Scottish coalfields and three from Kiverton Park returned to work today. Mr Scargill disputed the figures saying that only two miners returned to work. The rest were providing safety cover as the National Union of Miners has consistently covered.

Violence flared last night as police armed with batons and riot shields charged a peaceful picket. Several NUM members were taken for hospital treatment.

Following the police charge, police claimed they found a shotgun, although the exact location of the find was not disclosed.

Second trade union news (split group)

A statement was given from Congress House today claiming that the latest NCB figures for return to work amongst the miners were incorrect.

Also photographs taken of a shot-gun found in the vicinity of a picket line were shown by police today with the inference that it was to be used against them.

Today there are still 140,000 miners on strike after 9 months, and support groups all over the country have set up strike centre/soup kitchens to co-ordinate peaceful picketing.

Support for the strike is still strong amongst not only the mining communities, but the trade union and working class movement as a whole.

Third trade union news (from split group)

The trade union congress has strongly denied the claims by the National Coal Board of the return to work figures.

Arthur Scargill has said that reports coming from the coalfields were saying that there was gross police intimidation of his members both on and off the picket lines.

Police have said that a gun was found in a miner's home in the vicinity of Bilston Glen colliery.

First BBC news

Good evening. This is the 6 o'clock news. Tonight we have an up-to-the-minute report on the miners' strike.

Violence erupted outside Congress House this afternoon between miners and police. The violence seemed to be sparked off by statements made by the National Coal Board and police officials. Miners are angry at reports of the number of mines re-opening and their anger was fuelled by police accusations of firearms being used against them by miners.

The NUM leader Arthur Scargill today stated that none of his members were responsible for these actions and that no firearms had been used by anyone participating on the picket lines.

(A senior police officer) of the Metropolitan Police stated that they had conclusive evidence that a shot-gun had been used at the Bilston Glen picket line and that the weapon was in police hands.

Second BBC news

On a day that saw an increased drift back to work in particular at Bilston Glen by 12 coalface workers, further violence was taking place at Orgreave power plant resulting in police announcing the finding of a double-barrelled shot-gun near the plant. (A senior police officer) of West Yorkshire police said at a press conference that 'My officers are being subjected to extreme violence and I am concerned for their future safety'.

When asked for comment Arthur Scargill said 'Violence? The violence I see daily is being inflicted on my members by a politically motivated police force'.

The first trade union news has remarkable similarities with that produced by the police group. The key difference is in the ownership of the shot-gun which in the above news is left deliberately obscure. The second trade union group actually split on the question of who was said to be the owner of the gun. Some members of the group stated heatedly that the gun could not be said to belong to a miner. Those who held this view produced a news in which the police inferred 'that it was to be used against them'. When questioned, the authors of this commented that they intended this phrase to imply that the gun had been 'planted' as false evidence by the police. This view of the ownership of the gun turned out to represent quite a large body of opinion amongst these people as a whole. The final trade union news above was written by a single person from the second trade union group who believed that the gun should be linked to a miner (by which he meant a miner who was on strike).

Both of the 'BBC news' programmes portray the gun as being used in violent action against the police. The BBC groups contained most of the people who were personally unsure of the ownership of the gun or who believed that it belonged to a striking miner. The trade union groups contained a heavy representation of those who believed that the gun was owned by, or had been 'planted' by the police. These divisions of opinion were made clear in the answers to the formal questions.

The questions – the gun and picketing

The answers given on the origins of the gun contrast sharply with the views of the police officers in the last group. The largest body of opinion amongst the trade unionists believed the weapon was 'planted' as false evidence by the police. Seven believed this and one other person thought that it was a police weapon for potential use against the miners. One person actually believed it had been planted by the media to generate a sensational story angle. Of those who believed that it belonged to miners/pickets one believed that it was being used by a miner for the purpose of shooting rabbits for soup kitchens, three said that it belonged to striking miners and one that it was the property of a 'militant activist, not a miner'. Four people did not associate it with anyone in the strike and one gave the answer that it belonged to a working miner who was defending himself against striking miners.

These answers show something of the general disposition of the group to the strike and to the police who were often seen as the instigators of trouble where it had occured. There was also much criticism of television news, and the BBC (more than ITN) was seen by most as being 'right-wing', 'establishment', 'conservative', 'unfair', 'biased', and 'biased to the government'. One person thought that the BBC was 'middle-of-the-road' and one commended BBC2's news as being 'balanced'.

Despite the major differences between the views of this group and of the police officers, there was one area on which there was a shared perception. All of the trade unionists who had been to a picket line believed, along with the police, that picketing was largely peaceful. Just three in the group as a whole believed that picketing was mostly violent. The other sixteen people all believed that picketing was mostly peaceful. Of those who thought it violent, two gave television news as their source of information for this belief. The third had a brother who had been to the picket line and he based his views on what he had been told by him.

However, contact with people who had been at picket lines did not normally have the effect of making people believe that picketing was violent. Six people in this group who had not themselves been at the lines, stated that contact with miners and miners' wives support groups had convinced them that the media images were wrong. One person described her reactions on first seeing the violent images on the news and how she later came to change her mind.

> When I first saw the TV pictures I thought it was terrible because I thought it was really violent. Every time it came on I would just walk away and not watch it. Then most of my friends at work, their husbands are miners at Polkemmit Pit – they stood at the picket lines and there was never any violence, never any. The camera men must have deliberately filmed a violent bit for television.

There were other factors which had influenced people's rejection of the television images. Two of the group cited alternative information which had been provided by their union. There were two other reasons given which recurred again in later groups. The first was what one person spoke of as a 'general disbelief of the media' and the second was what amounted to a logical deduction. Two people stated that the scale of the picketing was such and the numbers involved in the strike so great, that there could not have been fighting most of the time. They had worked out that television was showing only 'small pockets' of trouble in a much wider pattern of events.

Most people in this group rejected the television news images as an accurate portrayal of picketing during the strike. But whether or not they believed what they had seen on TV, the whole group was convinced that news coverage of picketing had mostly consisted of such images. Views on this were so strong that 'picket-line violence' was estimated by the majority of the group to be the largest single issue covered in the news on the strike. This was partly because of the salience of the images and also because the issue was seen by many as a key feature of a 'biased' television presentation. But although these images were thought to have dominated the news, they were not the ones that stuck most in their minds.

Memories and beliefs

The memories which are strongest for most of the group related more to their obvious feelings for the miners. Here are the two sets of answers side by side:

	Question 7 (on news most)	**Question 8 (most personal impact)**
1	Arthur Scargill and miners' view of him	Scargill's arrest
2	Violence on picket lines	The miners struggle/fight against increased police patrols and how small communities fought through the strike together e.g. soup kitchens
3	Picket line violence/ degrading of Scargill	Miners' struggle/picket-line violence/degrading of Scargill
4	Violence and confrontation between miners and police	Government's bloody-mindedness to break miners no matter what the cost
5	Picket-line violence	Miners' families suffering/ death of a taxi-driver/ intimidation of non-strikers
6	Violence	Picket line and violence
7	Violence/return to work figures	Pro-strike miners' wives/ Arthur Scargill's stamina
8	Violence	Seeing men, women, and children suffer at the hand of government, police, and fellow trade unionists/police charges
9	Violence/Coal Board statements	Anti-union statements/bias against mineworkers' leaders
10	Arthur Scargill/violence	Very good impression of miners' (especially wives') tremendous support
11	Violent picketing/return to work figures	Bias against Scargill/media presentation of violence instead of support groups etc.

12	Violence/reports of meetings	Bias reporting of violence/ solidarity of women support groups
13	Violence on picket line	Hard-line attitude of NCB
14	Violence/working miners being brought into work	Police attacking defenceless people/policeman on horseback hitting woman in garden
15	Violence on picket line	Violence on picket line/Ian MacGregor being knocked down and the big thing that was made of this
16	More violence than anything	Innocent killing of taxi-driver taking miner to work
17	Picket-line violence	Picket-line violence on both sides, police and miners. Most striking was the way the police, who I thought of in terms of law and order, contributed to and started violence
18	Picket-line violence	Miners returning to work
19	Death of Welsh taxi-driver/ return to work figures	Mass police presence

There are some very interesting relationships which show up here. In the table of answers, the respondents numbered 6, 16, and 19 were the three people who believed that most picketing was actually violent. Their memories of the strike all involved violence and two of them name the death of 'the Welsh taxi-driver'. In this incident, during the strike, a taxi-driver was taking a miner to work and died when a concrete block was pushed on to the motorway by two striking miners. Inevitably such a disastrous event was also very damaging for the miners' cause and was covered extensively by television and the press.

If we compare these memories with those of the five people who were actually on picket lines and who were highly committed to the strike we can see a clear difference. These people are numbered 3, 8, 11, 12, and 14 and their sharpest memories all include themes of suffering and struggle by the miners.

The differences here show clearly how the information we

receive from the media can interact with our cultural values and experience to condition what we remember.

Conclusions

This group had largely disagreed with the views of the police officers on the causes of violence where it had occured. But there was a high level of agreement with the police on the generally peaceful nature of picketing. In order to test this correspondence further it seemed necessary to go to Yorkshire, which had been at the heart of the dispute and was the focus of much media coverage.

Miners, and women's support group, Yorkshire

This was a group of four miners and five women from a mining community in the heart of the Yorkshire coalfields. They were interviewed in July 1986, sixteen months after the strike had ended.

They included the local NUM branch secretary, a county councillor, and the chair, vice-chair, treasurer, and secretary of the Women's Action Group (the last of these was also a district councillor). All but one of this group had been on picket lines in areas which were extensively featured in media coverage. One of the men had been arrested during the strike and one had gone back to work before the dispute was over. Between them, this group had an extremely wide range of knowledge and experience of the events of that time.

Writing the news

The exercises were written in the local miners' club and the people formed two groups to produce a 'trade union news' and a 'BBC news'. Here is what they wrote:

Trade union news

> Arthur Scargill was at Congress House today talking about pit closures, and the known hit list. Ian MacGregor lied through his back teeth and denied that there was one. People turned up in their thousands on rallies showing their support for trade unionism.

Thousands of police and hundreds of pickets were at Orgreave today where (a senior police officer) contemplated using firearms against pickets.

BBC news

First breakthrough in hard-line Yorkshire.

Massed police with riot equipment faced massed pickets at (their local colliery). Three strikebreakers.

After police cleared pickets away shot-gun found on floor.

Chief Constable stated forensic evidence proved been fired in last 24 hours.

Evening. Police in riot gear went into (local miners' welfare club) to apprehend owner of shot-gun.

Large numbers arrested. Mass of locals outside local police station protesting.

MacGregor in interview stated this was evidence of revolutionary aspects in NUM.

Scargill leaving meeting of TUC stated that as no one had been arrested the gun could have been planted. 'How is it that with such vast numbers there, no one was hit (by the gun)?'

This group showed the same detailed knowledge of the dispute as had the police officers interviewed before them. Both they and the police were able to correctly name the senior police officer in the photograph they were using.

However, it is clear that the trade union news above differs from that written by the officers in the important area of the use of the shot-gun. In this version it is the police who are presented as contemplating the use of firearms. In the above 'BBC news' the gun *is* associated with the pickets. But the authors stated that this was what they thought the BBC would have said rather than what they themselves actually believed. All nine people in fact thought that the BBC news was either 'pro-government', 'right-wing', 'anti-union' or 'anti-working class'.[1] Consequently the BBC news produced by this group was close to being a parody. Even so the author's views do show through in the references to the possibility of the gun being 'planted'.

The questions – the gun and picketing

The strength of the views about where the gun should be located was shown in the answers given to question 1. Seven people believed that the police had either planted the gun or were about to use it in false evidence against the miners. The remaining two people thought that it was a poacher's gun, one believing that the poacher was a starving miner and the other thinking that he was simply someone who had been caught up in a picket area.

It was apparent from the group's comments that they felt a deep anger towards the police, who were seen as agents of the government in the breaking of the strike. One woman, who had a police officer as a close relative said that 'I used to bring my kids up to respect police. But I wouldn't tell them now to ask the police for help'. Eight out of the nine people said that their opinion of the police had changed markedly for the worse since the strike (the remaining one said that he had had a very negative opinion of them before it).

Yet these people all confirmed the view that had been given by the police that most picketing had been peaceful. In the cases where there had been trouble, they blamed the police for it. But even an area such as Orgreave, which was extensively featured in media coverage, was still judged by them to be mostly peaceful. The group also agreed with the police description of media coverage, which they believed had overwhelmingly featured picketing as violent.

Memories and beliefs

The first-hand experience which the group had of the dispute clearly affected their memories of the way in which it was featured in television coverage. Here are their answers to questions 7 and 8 put side by side.

	Question 7 (on news most)	**Question 8 (most personal impact)**
1	Violence on the picket lines/men returning to work	Vans and buses covered in wire mesh with large police escorts flying through picket lines

2	Scabs going into work/picket-line violence	The thing that most of all comes to mind about what was shown on TV was that they were trying to drive us back to work
3	Orgreave scab lorries	The bastard copper hitting a picket at Orgreave
4	Scab miners	Orgreave
5	Returning miners, the more the better	Policeman beating picket at Orgreave
6	Violence and charging on horses/miners returning by coaches	Charging police at Orgreave through the crowds – using truncheons on youths' heads
7	MacGregor, Scargill, and Tory ministers	Biased media coverage incriminating miners
8	Violence of the miners – any violence of the police was never actually shown	Orgreave, seeing for myself the lads around Orgreave, also the first morning the police vans arrived at [local colliery] to let in the scabs. [We] were there
9	Picket violence but cameras were never on the violence by police which caused it	Seeing my husband's car on the telly after the police had put weapons in his boot, also Orgreave

The estimates of what was shown most on the news are clearly affected by the intensity of the group's beliefs about the partisan nature of television news. They believed that the emphasis on miners returning to work in the media was a key element in weakening the strike. For the first person in the above list (who is actually the NUM branch secretary) the image of vans and buses flying through picket lines is the single dominant memory for the whole strike. The second respondent says simply that his memory of television is of it 'trying to drive us back to work'. As with the previous group of trade unionists, the coverage of violence is also seen as evidence of a partisan news treatment. Interestingly, the academic studies on this have now shown that there *were* many more references on the news to pits being 'open and working' than references to them being shut because of the strike action. As noted above, it has also been shown that violence was more frequently attributed to the miners and pickets than to the police (Cumberbatch *et al.*, 1986; Hetherington, 1985).

The intense personal involvement and actual experiences of this group at Orgreave and elsewhere clearly did affect their overall memories of the strike. Some were actually present at scenes which were then featured on television. This had both heightened their awareness and made them extremely critical of most news reporting.

Conclusions

This group shared the view expressed by other trade unionists and the police officers that most television news coverage of picketing had overwhelmingly focused upon violence. At the same time the group believed that in fact most picketing had been peaceful.

There is another group of workers who have a special interest in media products. We journey next to Fleet Street.

Print workers, Fleet Street

These were a group of nine workers employed in printing the *Daily Telegraph*. They were all in the National Graphical Association which is a traditional craft-based union. For many years this union had operated a strict closed shop and had successfully defended relatively high living standards for its workers. At the time of these interviews in April 1986, the union was involved in a series of major struggles. These were over the introduction and use of new print technology which involved the breaking of the closed shop. One dispute had already been lost in Warrington (over Eddie Shah's free sheet newspapers) and another major dispute was in progress with the owners of the *Sun* and *The Times*, now based in Wapping. The print workers in this group were not directly involved in these disputes but some had been picketing in Warrington and most of the group were about to go to the picket lines in Wapping. None had been on picket lines during the miners' strike, though it is clear that in some ways they identified themselves with the miners' cause. This is not to say that as a group they were politically 'radical'. Print workers such as these are more usually thought of as being highly paid, strongly committed to their union, and relatively conservative in their views.

Writing the news

A trade union and BBC group were established and no special preference was expressed by anyone to go in either group. Here is what they wrote:

> *BBC news*
>
> As the diagram shows, the NCB reports that miners are gradually drifting back to work in areas across the country. Mr MacGregor's opinion that the strike is crumbling is denied by Arthur Scargill and that the strike will carry on until the end.
>
> At Bilston Glen colliery there was a violent demonstration and many were arrested. Riot police later produced a shot-gun which they say was used against them.
>
> *Trade union view*
>
> In the third month of the miners' strike today at Bilston Glen it was reported 13 men returned to work, and a crowd estimated at 10,000 by the union, massed outside the main gates. The estimated police attendance was 8,000 in full riot gear.
>
> Following a massed charge by the police and led by (a senior police officer) 200 miners required hospital care.
>
> Among those arrested was miners' leader Arthur Scargill who after treatment at Bilston hospital was charged with carrying an offensive weapon, namely a shot-gun.
>
> At a news conference later in the day the miners' leader said it was impossible for him to conceal a shot-gun on his person and the police were obviously out to discredit him and his cause.

These examples were written about thirteen months after the strike ended but it can be seen how closely actual news phrases such as 'drifting back to work' are reproduced.

The placing of the gun in the story was the subject of much discussion in the groups. In the end it was placed with Arthur Scargill (in very suspicious circumstances) in the trade union news. The 'BBC news' reported that it was said to have been 'used against the police'. These formulations represent compromises between the complex attitudes to the media, the police, and other unionists which these workers actually held.

The questions – the gun and picketing

This group was generally very critical of the media (both newspapers and television news).[2] In their view of the BBC news, four people thought that it was 'establishment', three thought it was 'right-wing', one thought it was 'conservative' and one that it was 'left-wing'.[3] As a whole the group had also a very negative view of the police. Four said that their opinion of the police had markedly worsened since the miners' strike and five said that the events of the period had confirmed the negative view that they already held. Two of the group volunteered the information they had relatives in the police but said that this did not alter their attitude. The disputes at Warrington and Wapping in which their own union was involved seemed to have a profound effect on the group. One stated that 'I think I was a bit naive before' and another that 'We are paying the rates and they are doing this to us'.

But for all this level of criticism some of the group still apparently connected violence with the miners' 'side' of the dispute. In answer to the first question, two people believed that the gun belonged to a striking miner and one said that he thought it was in the news because a 'striking miner shot someone'.

There was another strand of opinion which was very revealing of how some in this group saw themselves. This was as 'respectable', rather than 'militant', trade unionists. In their replies three people made a distinction between the miners and what they regarded as less acceptable elements. In these replies the gun was said to belong to 'a radical left hanger-on', 'a left infiltrator', and 'a hanger-on with the pickets'. Of the remaining three people, two believed that the gun was planted by police and the last thought that it was an 'outsider wanting to discredit the miners'.

On the issue of whether most picketing involved violence, the group was virtually united. Eight stated that they believed picketing to have been mostly peaceful while one stated that he thought it involved 'emotional' if not physical violence. But they all believed that the television images of picketing had mostly been of violence.

None of these people had actually been to a picket line in the miners' strike. Yet they overwhelmingly rejected the television news account of what picketing was like. The reasons for this relate very much to their own position on Fleet Street. Six of the group made specific criticisms of the media saying, for example, that because of their own experience within it they 'don't believe what they read in the newspapers or see in the news'. They also commented that 'the media distorts' and that peaceful picketing was 'not news'. Two of these people made specific references to their own union's experience in Wapping saying that 'in Wapping most picketing was not violent' and 'there was picketing all the time but only the violence was shown'. Two people also noted that they had relatives or friends who were miners and this had influenced their judgement. One person also reached the same logical conclusion that we saw earlier with the Scottish trade unionists. He stated that it had to be mostly peaceful because 'if they had been really violent, the police couldn't have coped, it would have been the army'.

Memories and beliefs

Their memories of the miners' strike and beliefs about what was shown on the news are again influenced by a factor which is peculiar to their own position. It is their perception of themselves as trade unionists under threat. Here are their replies to questions 7 and 8:

	Question 7 (on news most)	**Question 8 (most personal impact)**
1	MacGregor's view	Wife and brick [through car window]
2	Nottinghamshire miners working	Horses and charge by police
3	People going back	People stopping coaches and cars up motorways
4	Drift back	Police tactics
5	Drift back	The day they lost – the disintegration of trade union solidarity
6	Coaches bringing miners back	Lorries moving coal, breaking picket lines, lorry after lorry

7 Miners working, going back to Nottinghamshire	Lorries bringing coal produced by working miners
8 Meetings	Police violence
9 Drift back	Destruction of trade unions and their collapse

There is an extraordinary emphasis here on the return to work with seven out of nine people believing this to be what was 'most shown' on television news. What is clearly in their mind is the disintegration of trade union solidarity which this represents. Four of them have this and the breaking of picket lines as their key memories of the strike. Two others have the police tactics in restricting picketing as what stuck most clearly in their minds. The case of the Nottinghamshire miners is especially poignant to them as an example of a division within a union, where a section of the workforce carried on working and, therefore, weakened the opposition to the employers. All this is obviously extremely relevant to their own anxieties about the use of 'black' labour or labour from other unions by employers in the print disputes.

Conclusions

The four groups discussed in this chapter offer several different perspectives on the miners' strike. Yet they shared some central beliefs in common. All believed that television news coverage of picketing had overwhelmingly shown violence, yet every person who had been to a picket line believed that picketing was mostly peaceful.

There were many reasons for the rejection of the media account, including direct experience, knowledge of miners and their families, and logical deductions based on the scale of picketing. The print workers rejected the media as information sources largely because their own work had given them a rather jaundiced view of the industry.

Another issue which became apparent with these groups was the extent to which people were able to mirror the style and in some cases the exact content of the news. It is important to see how widespread this ability was, especially given that the news exercises were being written over a year after the strike had actually ended.

All of the groups in this section were likely to have had special knowledge or experience of the strike. The next set of occupational groups are drawn from the more general population, beginning in a solicitors' office in the south-east of England.

3

Occupational groups

Solicitors' office, Croydon (south London)

This group consisted of most of the firm's employees including two solicitors, two legal executives, the book-keeper, and secretarial staff. They were interviewed in May 1986, fourteen months after the end of the strike. In the event, eight of the people were interviewed together and were divided into the usual groups. One person came later and was interviewed separately.

There were no special preferences expressed to go in either the BBC or the trade union groups.

Trade union news

At NUM headquarters at Congress House today Mr Scargill claimed that a peaceful demonstration by pickets was interrupted by the riot police in full riot gear, and many arrests made after scuffles.

The police alleged that rifle shots had come from the pickets. Mr Scargill disputed such claims saying 'this was a peaceful demonstration and it was quite clear that the demonstrators were completely unarmed' and suggested an outside agitator was the culprit. A police commissioner denied the allegations.

BBC news

Shot-gun found on picket line.

Today police discovered a shot-gun in a hut formerly occupied by pickets.

(A senior police officer) says 'an officer apprehended a miner in connection with this matter. We can assume it was his intention to use it during the disturbances'. Mr Scargill, when asked for his comments, replied 'this is pure conjecture by the officer concerned. This is another example of the pro-government, lackey police force'.

MacGregor, when asked for his comments, said 'I am not surprised because Mr Scargill has encouraged such behaviour by his inflammatory speeches'.

Both of these news programmes locate the gun with the pickets' 'side' in the dispute, although the trade union version also suggests that an outside agitator may be to blame. We can see how closely these accounts parallel the personal views of the authors.

The questions – the gun and picketing

Of the nine people interviewed, seven believed that the gun belonged to a striking miner or pickets and one other that it belonged to an 'outside trouble-maker'. The remaining person thought that it was the property of someone who was connected to the dispute but who was not actually a picket (e.g. a member of a miner's family or the police).

On the issue of violence in the strike there was a very clear division within this group as a whole, which in part related to differences in work experience. The secretarial staff believed that

13 Solicitors' office, Croydon

most picketing that had taken place in the strike was violent. But all the senior members of the firm including the solicitors, the book-keeper, and the legal executives rejected the media account and believed that most picketing was peaceful. Some of these people made very strong criticisms of both the media and the police which derived in part from their own professional contacts and experience. For example, one of the legal executives gave her experience in seeing court cases reported as her reason for rejecting television's portrayal of violence in the strike. In her words, 'the sensational bits are picked out'. More general criticisms of news reporting were also made, for example, that television would only show violence and 'dramatic shots of violence make better television'. Three of these people pointed to contradictions and differences between news reports as the reason why they had doubted television news. They compared coverage in the quality press with the more popular and sensational images of the strike.

We saw in the interviews with the trade unionists how a left-wing critique of television could lead to a rejection of the news as an information source. It is interesting that in this group some of the criticisms are coming from a more conservative perspective. For example, one of the senior members of the firm wrote that there was 'probably not as much violence as we are led to believe by TV news. News seems to sensationalize and exaggerate'. This was from a person whose preferred paper was the *Daily Telegraph* and whose key memory of the strike was 'workers' constant dissatisfaction with their lot – union trouble-making'. It is interesting that although this respondent's political views differed sharply from those of the trade unionists, there were nevertheless elements in common in the perception of how television news had presented violence.

Some of these judgements were clearly affected by professional and work experiences, but there were other influences which were much more random. For example, one of the group had a brother who was a policeman while another knew people who had been to a picket line, and these contacts had led both to believe that picketing was mostly peaceful. Two of the people also used logical processes to criticize news content, commenting that 'people couldn't be fighting all the time, twenty-four hours a day'. The *Daily Telegraph* reader, quoted above, stated that she sometimes noticed discrepancies between news reports while listening to the radio. These confirmed her belief that the news was exaggerated. For example, in a story about a disaster she noticed that initially a large number of people were reported to have been killed. But in later reports 'the numbers were whittled down'. On this she commented 'when you see that sort of thing you assume they all do it'.

Direct contacts with television personnel had also led to a jaundiced view of the medium. One person wrote that 'I know someone in HTV – I know that TV has to be full of "action" and, therefore, needs to show violence'.

Overall then, the senior members of the firm showed a very high level of criticism of television content. Interestingly, most of them (including the *Daily Telegraph* reader) believed that the BBC was biased in some way towards the right wing. Their comments were that it was 'slightly right-wing at present', 'slightly establishment', 'right of centre', 'pro-government of day'. One said that it was mostly 'impartial with some right-wing bias' and one that it was 'impartial'.

But this climate of opinion had clearly not embraced the secretarial staff who all believed that the BBC was 'impartial', 'neutral', or 'fair'. Everyone in the firm believed that the TV news presented picketing as mostly violent. But only the secretarial staff believed that these images represented what was typically happening. These people traced their own beliefs about picketing directly to the media. In answer to question 6, they wrote simply: 'TV and national press', 'press, bits of news on TV and people talking about it', 'TV news' and 'press and television'. The second of these answers says something about social interaction within the office as the people talking about the strike seem unlikely to have been the senior members of the firm. The newspaper sources to which they refer were *The Sun* for two of them and the *Daily Mail*.

In these cases, we can see how the beliefs on violence become part of an interlocking set of ideas, key elements of which are being provided by press and television. This is clearer if we look at a complete set of answers. For example, one of the secretarial staff wrote that she believed the gun belonged to striking miners; that BBC and ITN news were 'fair' (in the sense of being impartial) and that most picketing in the strike had been violent, as had the television portrayal of it. The sources for her beliefs about picketing were given as 'press and television', by which she meant the *Sun* newspaper and television news. She believed the subject shown most on the news was 'picket lines and Scargill' and what had stuck most in her mind was 'working miners and strikers fighting', and 'bitterness in families and friends'. Finally, her view of the police had improved as a result of what she had seen of the strike because as she said 'you do not realise what they have to put up with'.

But for other members of the same firm what was finally believed about the strike depended more obviously on experience and personal history. We might remember that one of those interviewed (a legal executive) had arrived late, because she had been in court that morning. Consequently, she was interviewed separately and wrote her own brief news story:

> *BBC news*
>
> Serious disruption and fear was caused by the police today at the coalmines, as a result of them using arms and threatening behaviour towards the pickets and the coal miners.

This is not a tongue-in-cheek news and the person stated that she believed the BBC to be 'impartial'. At the same time she rejected the view that most picketing in the strike had in reality been violent. From her professional experience she had seen the media concentrate on the sensational. At first sight then, we might see the news story as a radical critique of police practice since they are associated with 'threatening behaviour', 'using arms', and being 'disruptive'. But she had also written in her replies that her attitude to the police was 'quite positive' and she actually believed that the gun belonged to a striking miner. I asked her how she could reconcile these beliefs with what she had written in her news story. She replied:

> I understood that the police do things which are not 'by the book'. It wouldn't surprise me if an officer had picked up the gun and used it. Things which I have been told by police officers which they have done to people taken in for questioning might surprise some people, but in certain circumstances it would be understandable. I can see why they do it.

I asked her, if she saw the police in this way, why then did she describe them as causing 'serious disruption' in her news story? She replied:

> In the miners' strike, I did see the police as a disruptive force.

> I didn't feel that all those police officers should be sent in. The miners and pickets may have sorted it out between themselves. When I see the police I associate them with criminals and the miners are not criminals.
>
> I do have very mixed feelings, I do sympathize with the miners but I tend to see things from both sides. All my life I have had dealings with the police in my work and socially. My father was a police constable and my boyfriend was a CID officer.

The final comment about being a policeman's daughter comes almost like a punchline at the end to explain the complexity of her attitudes. Because she was so close to the police, she could both sympathize with them and know that they might sometimes break the rules. At the same time she had a very clear and professionally defined view of what police responsibilities are. Through this extraordinary set of filters she was able to envisage a situation in which the police might fire unlawfully at pickets, while retaining sympathy both for them and the miners. At the same time she used her professional background both to assess how the police should be used, and to reject the media account of what did occur in the actual events.

Memories and beliefs

The answers that the group gave to questions 7 and 8 are given here side by side. The first five respondents are the senior members of the firm and the last four are the secretarial staff.

	Question 7 (on news most)	**Question 8 (most personal impact)**
1	Picketing as far as I saw but I did get very bored after the first few months and switched off	Workers' constant dissatisfaction with their lot, union trouble-making
2	Police versus pickets confrontation – otherwise not good TV	Arthur Scargill/picture of the woman being struck or about to be struck by a mounted policeman – sadness that it seemed a total waste of time and effort

3	Clash between Arthur Scargill, MacGregor, and government	Total waste of time to glorify Arthur Scargill's own aims
4	Police and pickets clashing	Scargill in baseball hat giving press conferences on picket line
5	Pickets/picketing	Minicab driver being killed
6	Mostly violent picketing and personal stories of those involved	The *bitterness* between miners (families and brothers) striking and those not. These people being 'brothers' at work
7	Scargill	How long it went on for, amount of news coverage
8	Picket crowds and fighting	Police and injured pickets
9	Picket lines and Scargill	Working miners and strikers fighting – bitterness in families and friends

These answers show something of the variety of different sympathies which existed within the group as a whole. They varied from the description of the strike as being for the glorification of Arthur Scargill to feelings of sadness at the waste involved.

The responses also showed the sense of almost bewilderment with which some of the group viewed the emotions generated by the strike. The location in the south is interesting here. Most of the coalmining areas are in the north of England and in Wales and Scotland. This office in Croydon is in part of the south-east now associated with high wages, relatively frequent changes of job and 'dormitory suburbs' (from which commuters go to work in London).

In this solicitors' office I was told conversationally that one of the legal executives had just been 'head-hunted' from another business. In fact, in the period after these interviews both she and another member of staff then left to join different firms. In such a work situation there is not likely to be much sense of communal history.

It is not surprising then that some might find the intensity of the miners' struggle difficult to understand. This was not the only group in which there was a sense of shock at the bitterness of the strike and at sights such as young women with children shouting 'scab' at people who were their neighbours and 'brothers and work'. Of course there were people in the north who were saddened by the personal conflict and the break-up of families that the strike caused. But we are perhaps more likely to find in the south the sense of surprise that such intensity of feeling could be generated. It is interesting that none of the Scottish trade unionists or the miners themselves put the bitterness within the communities as their key image from the strike.

But there is not a complete cultural gap between the north and the south. There are some industrial areas and even a few coalmines in the south. Also, many people have moved in recent years from the north in search of higher living standards. It is thus quite possible to find in the south a sense of loss for closer communities as well as a more general distaste for what is seen as the commercial priorities and pressured living in London. There was thus a potential level of sympathy in the south for the miners and their communities. Media coverage of the strike may have lessened this potential support by its focus on violence and by making 'picket lines and fighting' key associations with the strike. For many of the groups discussed here, these images seem to have overwhelmed memories of what else was shown.

Conclusions

We can now see some clear patterns emerging of the possible effects of media content on belief. Some of this group had access to alternative information sources or had used professional experience or logic to question the prevailing images of violence. But where such sources of criticism were lacking, there was a much higher probability of belief in the media. Amongst some of the group we could see tightly organized sets of beliefs, central elements of which were being provided by the press and the television news.

It was important to know how these processes might be affected by differences in political culture or regional area. This office was situated in a commercial business centre in the heart of the south-east. To provide a contrast with this we go now to a solicitors' office in Glasgow.

Solicitors' office, Glasgow

Glasgow and the west of Scotland are associated with traditional industries and a political culture which is more radical/left-wing than that of the south-east of England. This is partly because of the historical concentration of heavy industry in the area and the development of a working-class politics which goes back at least to the turn of the century and to the time of the 'Red Clyde'.

A second dimension is the relationship with England which is still perceived by many as a dominant, even colonizing, power. It is the Conservative strongholds of the south-east of England, and the Westminster parliament in particular, which are seen as the source of this power. These feelings were given considerable impetus by the discovery in the 1970s of oil off the Scottish coast. Nationalists then saw this as being exploited for the benefit of the English. The Scottish National Party slogan was for many years 'It's Scotland's oil'.

A third and crucial factor has been the rise in unemployment over the last twenty years and the decline in industries such as steel, shipbuilding, and coal. Because of this national dimension, the decline is seen as an issue for Scotland rather than as simply a problem for the working class. Consequently, the climate of popular radicalism has actually spread into the middle classes. In the general election of 1987, there were no Conservative MPs elected at all in the city of Glasgow. Even a very middle-class area, such as Bearsden and Strathkelvin, which is the equivalent of the dormitory suburbs of London, elected a Labour MP. Such a climate has sustained a Scottish press which is by English standards very radical. Illustration 14 is from the Glasgow *Evening Times*, which is one of the largest papers in Scotland, and shows their front page the day after the 1987 election.

Writing the news

The firm of solicitors in Glasgow was larger than the previous one and specialized in property, tax and company law. It was situated in a very extensive office complex in the centre of the city. In all eighteen people took part, including secretarial and catering staff, trainee and qualified solicitors, and five senior partners. The bulk of this group were interviewed on an initial visit to the firm and the five partners were seen on a separate visit shortly afterwards. The first group produced two 'BBC news' programmes and what was termed a 'Channel 4/Alternative trade union news'. The partners then produced a third 'BBC

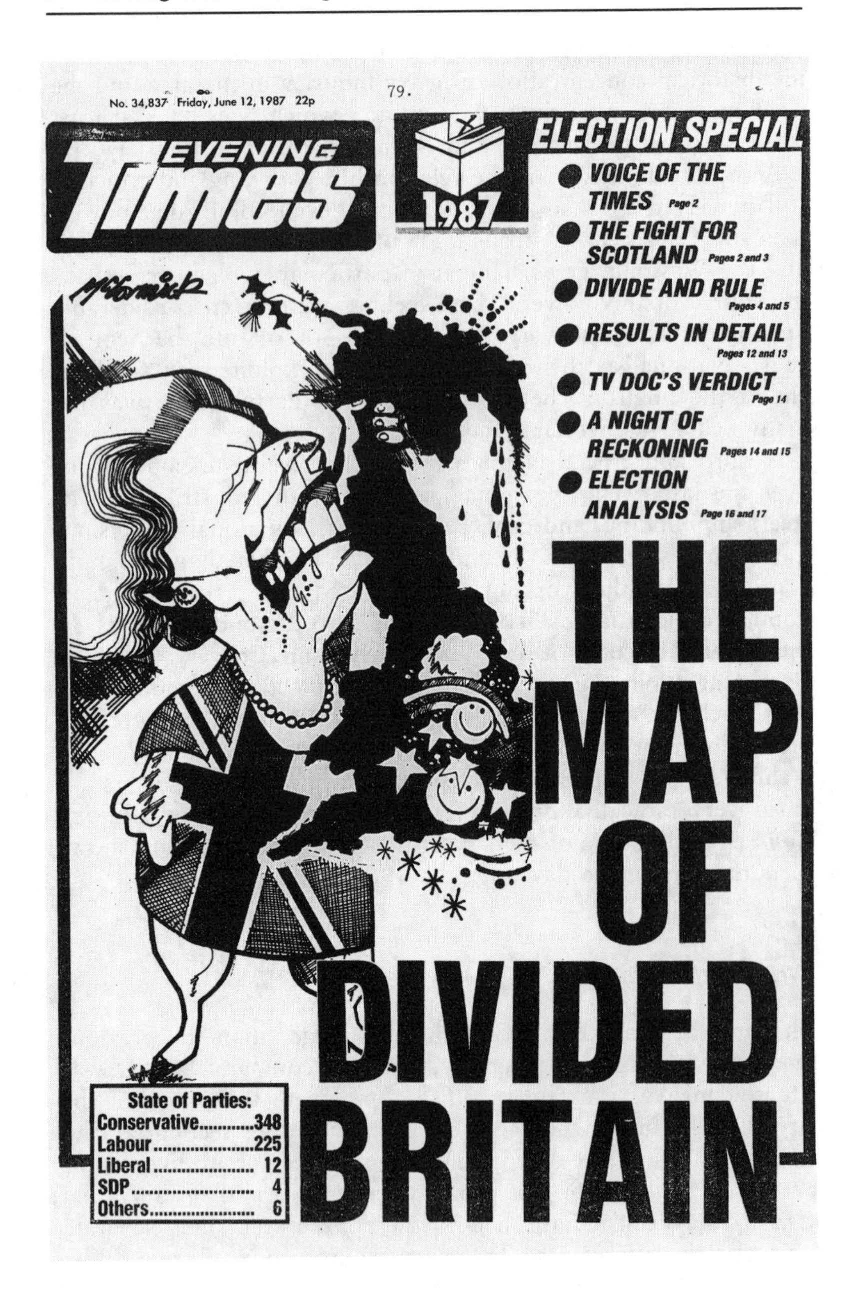

No. 34,837 Friday, June 12, 1987 22p

79.

EVENING Times

ELECTION SPECIAL

1987

- VOICE OF THE TIMES Page 2
- THE FIGHT FOR SCOTLAND Pages 2 and 3
- DIVIDE AND RULE Pages 4 and 5
- RESULTS IN DETAIL Pages 12 and 13
- TV DOC'S VERDICT Page 14
- A NIGHT OF RECKONING Pages 14 and 15
- ELECTION ANALYSIS Page 16 and 17

McCormick

THE MAP OF DIVIDED BRITAIN

State of Parties:	
Conservative	348
Labour	225
Liberal	12
SDP	4
Others	6

14 The *Evening Times*, 12 June 1987

news'. There was no preference expressed by anyone to go in a particular group. Here is what they wrote:

First BBC news

The long-running mining strike today appeared to be reaching a conclusion. Arthur Scargill, the miners' leader, today left Congress House refusing to comment on Ian MacGregor's statement on television last night that the floodgates were beginning to open with miners now returning to work at increasing rates every day.

Mr MacGregor referred to today's NCB report that thirteen more miners had returned to work at the Scottish pits with three returning to work at Kiverton Park. Two reasons were given by Mr MacGregor for this move towards return:

Firstly, the increasing violent clashes between pickets and police. Today one man was arrested for possession of a shot-gun on the picket line at (a colliery).

Secondly, he quoted the increased hardship on the part of the miners families. Despite fund and moral raising events within the miners' welfare clubs, the financial hardship, he said, was now becoming too much for many families.

Second BBC news

Trouble broke out between police and miners today at a colliery in Bilston Glen. There were many arrests.

Amongst the weapons confiscated there was a sawn-off shot-gun.

The miners leader, Arthur Scargill, said that there were National Front supporters mingling with the demonstrators who provoked the crowd.

Ian MacGregor was later reported to have said that the whole episode was a publicity stunt.

Channel 4/Alternative trade union news

As miners and their families gathered in Rochdale to listen to Mr Scargill they were met by police in riot gear. As numbers swelled police called in reinforcements and in the face of such provocation, ugly scenes erupted.

After the trouble had died down a shot-gun was produced by

the police, which they claimed had been taken from the mob. A senior policeman said 'In the face of such intimidation my officers had no alternative but to meet the threat head on'.

Mr Scargill, the president of the NUM, condemned the police reaction as completely unwarranted and said 'this was peaceful meeting attended by the wives and children of the miners, as your cameras will bear out'.

Mr Ian MacGregor refused to comment.

Undeterred by the events of the day the miners and their families met up later in the day in the Community Hall when in a show of solidarity with their colleagues, they held a concert for the benefit of the families.

Third BBC news

More trouble on the picket lines today. Police were out in force at Bilston Glen where 12 miners have now returned to work.

Police wore full riot gear as the bus containing strikers drove through the gates.

There were ugly scenes and when the police went in to make arrests a shot-gun was found. The chief constable expressed deep concern over what was said to be an alarming escalation of violence.

Meanwhile, against a background of no movement between the parties to break the deadlock, Sir Ian MacGregor questioned how negotiations could be expected to take place in a climate of escalating violence.

A grim-faced Arthur Scargill left Congress House this evening without comment after being told that talks had broken up again.

These stories were written about sixteen months after the strike had ended. They show the ability of the people to reproduce the basic themes as well as the detailed language of news reports. The descriptions of the return to work, for example, are in fact very close to actual news text. It is especially interesting that they can be produced so long after the strike ended, on the basis of a small number of relatively ambiguous photographs.

The pictures seemed to trigger a flow of memories and associations in the groups.

The ambiguity of the pictures meant that they could be used in different ways according to the beliefs and assumptions of the writers. For example, when the third 'BBC news' was being written one of the group picked up the picture of a crowd of people standing and sitting around at a public meeting. He then suggested for a story: 'They drove through the angry mobs'. A second person in the group commented: 'That doesn't look like an angry mob to me'. The first replied, 'Oh, these ones here don't look too happy'.[1]

The placing of the gun in the stories is also noteworthy. It is largely associated with the pickets' 'side', though in one story there is the implicit suggestion that it may be linked to National Front supporters. This reflects the views of one of the group, though the bulk of these people did in fact believe it was a miner's/picket's weapon.

The questions: the gun and picketing

In the group as a whole, thirteen believed that the gun belonged to the miners/pickets. Of the rest, one thought it belonged to a quick reaction police force, one to a working miner, one to thugs/left-wing agitators who had infiltrated the union, one to a trouble-maker, and one to a National Front 'freak'. About a third of this group actually expressed some clear sympathy with the miners, but even with these people, three still associated the gun with striking miners and/or picket lines. One of these was a trainee solicitor who read the *Guardian*, watched 'alternative Channel 4 documentaries', and whose beliefs about the police had changed because she was 'worried at the Force's ability to become increasingly militarized'. She stated that she was sympathetic to the miners and said that the connection she had made with the gun probably came, in spite of her beliefs, from what she had seen on television news. Neither she nor any of the others in this group had actually been on a picket line or had been actively involved in supporting the strike. She commented:

> I thought that the gun was the type of thing they would have shown and that it had been taken from a picket.

This is an important example since it shows that the associations made by television news between violence and the miners seem to have been absorbed even where people have critical attitudes on the specific issue.

As a whole this group were doubtful about the neutrality of television, especially of the BBC. Six of them said that the BBC was 'pro-government', 'Conservative', 'right-wing'; five that it was 'slightly right-wing' and four that it was 'pro-establishment'. Only three said that they believed it to be 'balanced' or that it 'told the truth'. In part these beliefs came from the perception of the BBC as reflecting the views of the south of the country. As one person put it the BBC has 'an establishment viewpoint, following the status quo – the majority view in south-east England'. This view of the BBC was shared by some of the group who described themselves as being politically to the right. Indeed one respondent said that she preferred to watch the BBC which she described as 'right-wing' because she was herself 'slightly to the right'.

Everyone in the group believed that most of what television news had shown of picketing had been violent. But this was rejected by the bulk of this group as an accurate view of what had typically happened. Only three out of the eighteen people believed that picketing had been mostly violent and one person was unsure. The main factor in this rejection of television news seemed to be cynicism about it as a reliable source of information. Eight of the group gave this as a reason, pointing, for example, to the news values of television to explain why it might exaggerate violence. Many had used other sources such as the quality press or local news reports to criticize the television images. One of these noted that:

> If you watch the first two minutes of news you would have the impression that it was pure violence – unless you watched more and read in far more depth.

Another offered a very interesting internal critique of the television images:

> You don't necessarily believe everything you see. They would focus on violent incidents, but when you looked at it you could see that there were lots of other people, where nothing was happening.

Another commented that:

> News coverage has the effect of making something look worse than it is. Is it not generally thought that television will do this?

These eight people were all sceptical about news coverage. But it was still for them their main source of information since they had no direct or indirect experience of the strike. Although they rejected the view that most picketing had been violent, it is still very interesting that half of them estimated the incidence of violence in the strike to be very high. One said, for example, that there was 'a lot of violence, but not mostly violent'. To this extent the media images did apparently have some influence on their perception of the strike.

But in the rest of the group there were people who had more direct experience of the events or of those involved. They were not, therefore, relying on the media as a key source of information. These people were much more likely to simply reject the television images. One, for example, knew a miner's family, and another knew a policeman, and both said that these contacts had influenced their views.

In another instance, a solicitor wrote that he had driven past a picket line during the strike whilst on a routine journey. He had seen that this was peaceful and had then compared it with the television images. In a similar vein one of the secretaries wrote that she had once worked at Chrysler while a strike was in progress. She said that picketing in this had been most peaceful and she had regarded the media coverage of this dispute as very unrealistic. She used this experience to reject the TV news presentation of the miners' strike. In this group as a whole, four people had direct experience of being at or near picket lines (without being directly involved). This raises an important regional difference between this group and the one in Croydon. In Britain nearly all mines and most heavy industry are concentrated outside the south-east. It therefore seems possible that people in the north will be more likely to have seen miners' picket lines or to have indirect experience which might affect perceptions of media coverage.

Several people in this group also used logic as a basis for questioning television reports. Five gave answers which mentioned the numbers involved in the strike. One person noted that it is a 'common-sense deduction that although TV shows violent incidents it does not follow that such incidents are widespread'. Another commented that 'they couldn't gather up so much momentum all the time, there had to be times when it was just day-to-day'.

There was one other reason given, which appeared here for the first time. It was the moral belief that most people do not act in a violent way. One woman commented that she 'believed most people *are* peaceful'.

Just three people in this group believed that picketing was mostly violent. In the Croydon office, there were several examples of people with tightly organized sets of ideas, strongly influenced by the television news and the press. It was possible to find this in the Scottish group but it seemed much rarer. One secretary, for example, wrote that the gun belonged to 'a striking miner left behind after riot', and that 'picketing mostly involved trouble – assumed this by what was seen on TV'. She thought that what had been shown most was 'fighting between police and miners/Arthur Scargill' and her key memory of the strike was the 'taxi-driver being killed taking a non-striking miner to work'. Her sympathy for the police had increased since the strike. This corresponds with the examples from Croydon, except that she believed the BBC to be 'slightly towards the right'.

A member of the catering staff had similar views on picketing. She wrote that the gun belonged to a picket, the BBC and ITN told the 'truth', and picketing was mostly 'trouble'. She thought that what had been shown most was 'violence with pickets and miners at work, blacklegs'. But her key memory of the strike was the 'loss of money and break-up of families, fathers and sons'. Her source of information was given as 'newspaper and TV' and her attitude to the police hadn't changed. She was the only person in this group to mention loss of money, which was probably not unrelated to the level of her own earnings. This is an important point, since, as we will see in other groups, class experience can have important influences on what is remembered.

The third person with these views on picketing was an audio typist, who gave a very complex response. She believed the gun belonged to a working miner and that both the BBC and ITN were 'slightly right-wing'. She thought that picketing involved 'a lot of violence actually going on' and her source for this was 'watching television'. She believed that what had mostly been shown was violence, but her key memory of the strike was 'police charging miners'. Her opinion of the police had changed for the worse because of them 'showing pay slips to miners, intimidating the miners'. The papers which she read were all Scottish, the *Evening Times*, *Daily Record*, and *Glasgow Herald.*

Overall this does suggest that attitudes to television news were more generally critical in the Scottish group and even where some of the television message was accepted, the belief was more likely to be accompanied by critical elements.

Memories and beliefs

These indicate the wide range of opinion on the strike and attitudes to the police which were present in the firm. Here are the answers to questions 7 and 8 put side by side:

	Question 7 (on news most)	**Question 8 (most personal impact)**
1	Police/miners confrontation/violence towards blacklegs	Victimization by police of 'unresisting' miners/police horses charging/horrific weapons used
2	Violent incidents between police and pickets	Picket-line violence against police/bricks at lorries on motorways etc.
3	Police violence and police handling of miners	Police horses charging in a line (charge of the light brigade)
4	Interviews with leading personalities (Scargill and MacGregor) scenes from picket lines	Killing of taxi-driver
5	Violence on picket line	Inflexibility of Arthur Scargill/violence against other miners/taxi-driver killed
6	Picket-line demonstration against working miners and police	Concrete block, motorway case incident
7	Fights between police and miners/Arthur Scargill	Taxi-driver being killed taking a non-striking miner to work

8	Violence shown mostly	Police charging miners
9	Clashing between miners and police	Arthur Scargill blasting anyone who had a view which did not accord with his own
10	Ian MacGregor/Arthur Scargill interviews	The miner's wife who drove her husband to work and the car was stoned
11	Violence	Margaret Thatcher's involvement in the dispute
12	Violence on picket lines and also the so-called 'blacklegs'	I really thought a lot about the 'blacklegs' and the treatment they received. I felt freedom of choice is a personal thing and prosecution for your choice is totally unfair
13	Violence with pickets and miners at work, blacklegs	Loss of money and break-up of families, fathers, and sons
14	Confrontation between police and pickets	Conflict between NCB and employees which could not be resolved – reluctance of NCB to negotiate honestly
15	Negotiation making no progress	Arthur Scargill
16	Picketing	The busloads of returning strikers and lorries going through the pickets
17	Picketing	Intimidatory picketing
18	Crowd scenes/people leaving or arriving at meetings	Police in riot gear/cynical manipulation of masses by both sides

The replies numbered 1 to 6 were from solicitors and trainee solicitors. Those from 7 to 13 were from the secretarial staff plus the one member of the catering staff. The last five answers were from the senior partners in the firm. The list shows the extraordinary impact of the violent images with fifteen out of the eighteen saying that they believed violence or picketing to be what was shown most on television news. For eleven of the people these images carried across to what had affected them most.

The list also shows how feelings of sympathy for the miners existed at different levels in the firm, as did criticisms of the strike. The people who expressed sympathy either in written answers or in interviews are numbered in the list as 1, 6, 8, 11, 14, and 16. It is interesting that only one of these people names the death of the Welsh taxi-driver as a key memory of the strike and she does not use the word 'killed' but refers to it as the 'motorway case incident'. There was in fact an extensive debate at the time over whether the death was intentionally caused, in which case it should be classified as murder, or whether it was not, in which case it was manslaughter. It can be seen that the people who are not particularly sympathetic to the striking miners use the word 'killed'. It does indicate how values can structure our memories and the specific language with which we remember events.

This was also shown in the group's attitudes towards the police. Here we find that a mixture of belief and personal experience is sometimes used to interpret images from the strike. In the group as a whole nine people said that their attitude to the police had become worse since the strike and one said that his view of them was already negative. Two people said there was no change in their views and six said that they were now more sympathetic to the police, saying, for example, that they 'recognized the police have a harder job' or that 'it must be a rotten job at times'.

Of the people who now had a more negative attitude to the police, half of them quoted personal experiences. These were then sometimes related alongside their view of events in the strike. For example, a solicitor wrote that his attitude had changed because of:

> experience of friends being victimized – friend picked up whilst drunk, being beaten up and then it being said he had fallen down stairs. During the miners strike, picking on less resistant miners.

One of the secretarial staff wrote:

> The police harrassment I saw on TV. They couldn't handle large crowds of people all at once. Boys in school picked on by police, beaten where people couldn't see the bruises.

Sometimes the connection was less direct. Another solicitor

wrote that he no longer viewed the police as just the 'bobby on the beat'. Their role could now be more 'physical within the community and also appear to be used in a political role in complex situations'. Having gone so far, he then made a special insertion to add:

> I am in the Territorial Army and spoke with police commissioners from Dumfries and was impressed with their common sense, their experience and their ability to do a difficult job. *But* there can be 'bad police'.

He then gave a detailed example of what he saw as police abuse involving his own family. This response seems to reflect an uneasy tension between (1) the pre-existing belief (the bobby on the beat), (2) the negative experience, and (3) the information being received from the media about the strike.

By contrast, another respondent, who was a senior partner, simply used the events of the strike to confirm a pre-existing view. He wrote that his attitude had changed:

> To the extent that my cynicism about the police being an arm of government policy rather than being an independent law enforcement agency has hardened.

It is interesting that even with such a firm commitment, this person still associated the gun with the striking miners.

Conclusions

There were some important differences between this group and the one in the Croydon solicitors' office. This firm dealt largely in property, tax and company law, so there was no reference to court experience as a way of evaluating media coverage.

An important factor in this group's assessment of television news was the different political culture which exists in Scotland. There was some clear support for the miners cause expressed in this group and the majority saw the BBC as being to the right of the political spectrum. This, plus the use of logic and local experience, led to criticisms of television images. Some experiences were in part related simply to geography. Several people in this Scottish group had been at or near locations of industrial conflict (without being actually involved).

There is a final point to be made on political culture. There was not in Glasgow the level of hostility and almost agitation that existed in parts of the south at the mention of Arthur Scargill. It was certainly not the case that everyone in this group approved of the miners' leader. But even disapproval seemed at times to be conditioned by a kind of cultural knowledge and closeness. As one of the senior partners remarked: 'I could see what Scargill was up to, I wanted him to be duffed'. Cultural history and experience can clearly have some effect on perception and belief in news content. To look at this further we now return to the south, to interview a group of black women in London Transport.

London Transport workers – catering staff

This was a group of seven black women working in a large canteen in Central London. They had no advance knowledge of the exercise and agreed simply to be taken off their shifts for a short period, two or three at a time. In the event, I explained what the exercise was, they looked at the photos, talked about them for a few minutes and then dictated the stories to me. I was asked to write the stories down as their hands were messy from

15 London Transport catering staff

the canteen work. This spontaneity is important since they apparently did not have to think very hard about the subject, even though this was fourteen months after the strike had ended. They all produced 'BBC news' programmes:

First BBC news

Good evening, here is the news. The miners' strike. The Coal Board manager, Ian MacGregor, has not yet come to terms with the miners' leader, Arthur Scargill, about the pit closures.

There was a disturbance involving the police and miners. The police were defending non-striking miners, those on strike defended themselves by throwing missiles. As a result of that the police used guns to control the crowd.

Second BBC news

Good evening. This is the news about the miners' strike, concerning the pit closures. There were pickets outside the coal-mine to prevent lorries going in with coal and coming out, and to prevent men going in to work.

Policeman were called to keep them off the gate so that they could unload the lorries and let some of the men who wanted to work get in.

The gun was an exhibit which was found on the strikers and produced by the police.

Third BBC news

Tonight Mr Scargill has called for a vote of confidence in the miners. It was voted 2 to 1 for the strike.

Mines were picketed, coal was stopped from getting out. Violence actually broke out with the police on the scene. There were shots from the crowd, people were panicking.

A chief of police arrived on the scene and told his men: 'This is Britain, find the person who fired the shot'.

The stories show how some key themes have stuck in the authors' minds: the arguments between MacGregor and Scargill over pit closures, the conflict between working and striking miners, and the movement of coal through picket lines. The placing of the gun in relation to the police is also very important. In the first story the police are actually firing weapons and the second story is intended to carry the implication that the weapon has been planted. As one of the authors commented, the 'police presented it that it was found on the strikers'. The third group was split over the ownership and it is left ambiguous in their story. These attitudes were made clearer in the answers to the questions.

The questions – the gun and picketing

The gun was very strongly associated with the police. Five out of the seven people believed that it was owned by the police either for use, or that it had been 'planted as evidence'. The other two believed it belonged to the crowd or militants.

Their attitudes to the BBC and ITN were largely that they 'told the truth' and were 'balanced'. But one commented that the BBC was 'for the government' and another that 'sometimes they just make things up for the government'. On the general issue of picketing they all believed that most of what had actually taken place was violence and fighting. Not surprisingly, they all believed that most of what they had seen of picketing on television news was violent. It was this in fact that had mostly informed their beliefs. Four said that television was their main source, two others included newspapers (*Daily Mirror* and *Daily Express*) in addition to television, and one included radio.

Memories and beliefs

These are again dominated by the images of violence and fighting, mixed with sympathy for the suffering which was caused. The answers to questions 7 and 8 are again put side by side:

	Question 7 (on news most)	**Question 8 (most personal impact)**
1	Police and riots	People (pickets) being carried with head wounds and blood
2	Miners, police fighting	How police were treating miners
3	Violence	Men going back (at end of strike) – I shed tears; women cooking
4	Violence	Violence, fighting

5 Picketing/scuffling	Families suffering
6 Picketing/Scargill	Violence, soup kitchens, families torn apart
7 Picketing	Violence, the families

This heavy associations of the strike with violence does relate in some way to their reliance on the popular press and television news for information. But their attitudes are made more complex by their concern about the police. No one in the group said that their attitude to the police had improved since the strike. Two people said that their attitude had not changed and one said that the police were 'just doing their job'. But this person had in fact associated the gun with the police and her key memory of the strike was given as 'how police were treating miners'. The remaining four people said that their attitudes to the police had become much more negative since the strike and other events which had followed it such as the inner-city riots of 1985. One woman for example commented that she was now 'more worried about the police since [the riots]. I have to keep the children indoors all the time'. She also commented of the miners' strike that 'the strikers were not violent – it was the police who forced it on them. We have one of them [situations] like that now behind us at Wapping'. This last reference was to the print dispute which was still in progress. It was the same dispute in which the print workers from Fleet Street were involved. The link that the respondent makes between the miners' strike, the inner-city riots, and the print dispute at Wapping is very interesting. She had never been to a picket line and gives television as the source of her belief that most picketing is violent. Yet she has clearly used other experiences to inform her belief that the police were responsible for the violence. The rest of her answers corresponded to this view. For example, she believed that the gun belonged to the police, but that it was 'presented' by them as belonging to the miners. She was also rather dubious about television news, believing that both the BBC and ITN were 'for the government'.

But for others in the group, their concern about the police created much more tension between different elements of their own beliefs. We could look, for example, at the two women who associated the gun with 'the crowd/militants'. The newspapers which they read were the *Sun* and the *Daily Express*, both of which are editorially very conservative. The reader of the *Daily Express* commented while preparing her news item that 'there's a lot of militants about'. She believed that what had mostly been shown on the news, apart from picketing, was Arthur Scargill. Both of these women had worked on the same news items which had featured the chief of police saying 'This is Britain, find the person who fired the shot'. This was meant in the sense that this sort of thing shouldn't happen here. But a few moments later in the interview, one of the women commented that her attitude to the police had changed because

> During the Tottenham riots, the police kicked down our door and beat up my brother.

The other woman, the *Daily Express* reader, also commented that

> I used to feel safe when I saw a policeman – not any more.

Such views of the police can clearly carry across to how other events are seen and remembered. So, although the first of these women associated the gun with the pickets she also said that picketing was mostly violent because the crowd were 'provoked by the police'.

Conclusions

Two issues stand out with this group. Firstly, the gun and violence are strongly associated with the police. Secondly, all of them believed that picketing was mostly violent and ascribed this belief to what they had seen in the media. But the perception of the police had clearly affected the views of some on the origins of violence.

It is sometimes argued that the media have little effect on belief and that most people believe that television and the popular press will exaggerate and perhaps distort. There were certainly people in this group who felt this, yet they had taken some of their key assumptions about the strike from what they had seen. At the end of these interviews, I read out the descriptions of picketing that had been given by the police, the miners, and the other trade unionists. These were greeted with real surprise. As one woman commented,

> People always say don't believe what you hear in the media, but this really gives you something to think about.

While I was at London Transport, I was given the opportunity to interview a group of catering supervisors. They were attending a short training course on the same day as the interviews with the canteen staff.

London Transport canteen supervisors

There were six people in this group, aged in their 20s and all white. By London standards they would be relatively low-paid. They divided into two groups with no preference for either a 'BBC' or trade union news. The programmes which they produced took the form of short histories of the strike, as if a series of news clips were being shown to illustrate the events of the period. Here is what they wrote:

BBC news

> Today Coal Board management and union met at Congress House over pit closures and the re-shaping of the industry. After a lengthy debate between Mr MacGregor and trade union boss Mr Scargill, talks again broke down and a strike is on the cards.
>
> Meetings were called at local and national level. National executive called for strike, majority said yes, but no ballot was taken.
>
> Strike starts.
>
> Pits were closed but some remained working. Pickets started peacefully, few police in attendance.
>
> Strike continues after lengthy meeting broke down yet again.
>
> Strikers become more militant, more police needed to control large amounts of pickets. Violence started on picket lines. Weapons started to appear, mostly against miners that were working.
>
> Amongst weapons found were a shot-gun and rocks and stones, but police were investigating whether the gun was going to be used.

Fund-raising events were held throughout the strike to support miners on strike.

After one year on strike, miners are slowly returning to work.

Trade union news

MacGregor says closures to come to uneconomic pits.

Mines looked to be closing down.

Meetings were held at local trade union levels and then at branch levels.

Scargill was called in to help negotiations. Meetings with MacGregor were held at TUC headquarters.

Talks broke down.

Scargill called strike action.

Due to change of law, no secondary picketing allowed.

Police were called in to control pickets. Head of Yorkshire Police called in to answer allegations of police violence as the picketing escalated. Violence was so bad that some members stepped outside the law (gun picture).

Negotiations continued to fail and after a year miners started to return to work.

These examples show again how specific themes in the dispute, such as the protracted negotiations and the slow return to work, are retained in people's memories. They also show how these memories reflect very much the Government and Coal Board's view of this dispute. For example, the central issues are taken to be 'uneconomical pits' and 're-shaping of the industry'. But the NUM did not accept the Government's analysis of which parts of the industry were 'economical' and saw the conflict as a calculated attack upon the union. As we shall see, the Coal Board's view runs through the accounts of several groups, including those sympathetic to the miners. In the above news stories the gun is again associated with pickets/union members. It is interesting that in the trade union news, the authors are familiar enough with union procedures to refer to meetings at local and branch level and to use the term 'members', but they then present their own side as stepping outside the law.

The questions – the gun and picketing

By contrast with the previous group, no one here believed that the gun belonged to the police. Three people thought that it belonged to striking miners, one to militant miners/infiltrators and two people did not associate the gun with anyone in the strike.

Only one of this group believed that the BBC was 'impartial'. Three thought that it 'veers towards right-wing', was 'right-wing', or was 'pro-government'. One said that it was 'biased sometimes' and one did not watch it.

The group all believed that television news had mostly portrayed picketing as being violent, but they were split evenly over whether or not it had in reality been mostly peaceful. One rejected the media account because he believed that 'the media blow up any incident wrongly – they are there to sell news or papers'. This general critique of the media was given a more political edge by another respondent who wrote that 'I think they picked out the violence so as to get the majority of people against the miners'. The third person rejected the television account because it 'tends to show the bad parts'. He based this view on his friendship with a policeman and his family, who had given him a more direct view of what picketing was like.

Three people believed that picketing had in fact been mostly violent. Two of these based their views directly on television and the press. The other person had stayed for a period in Selby, Yorkshire, and had thought that the attitudes of the local people were very 'them and us'. From this he had assumed that picketing was more likely to be 'fiery' and not mostly peaceful. Neither he nor anyone else in this group had actually been to a picket line.

Memories and beliefs

Their beliefs about what was shown most on the news are very close to those of the previous group.

	Question 7 (**on news most**)	**Question 8** (**most personal impact**)
1	Fighting and aggression	The arrogance of Arthur Scargill

2 Non-peaceful picketing and miners' lives	Divided union and families
3 People trying to get to work but not able	Break-up of families, striking and non-striking/violence, taxi-driver killing
4 Violence/hate	Fight for power of workers over management
5 Violence involved and how hard it was for the miners' families	Violence and grief caused to both sides, miners and their families and police
6 Violence on picket lines	Taxi-driver being killed, bitterness

The key memories of the strike included several references to the break-up of families, bitterness, grief, and hate. The sense of surprise and perhaps shock at such intense emotions seems to be a response which occurs more frequently in the South.

There are no references to police action and in response to a direct question on attitudes most of the group said that their views had not changed since the miners' strike. Two said that their opinion had changed – one believing that the police should now be 'more accountable' to the general public and the other saying that there were 'some bad apples in all parts of society'. These responses as a whole contrast quite sharply with those of the previous group.

In both of the London Transport groups it did seem that television and the press were having some impact on beliefs. It was also clear that the messages were in some ways re-negotiated and the final beliefs of the individuals often contained tensions and contradictions. However, in the supervisors' group there was an interesting example of a person who apparently had a relatively untroubled perception and whose beliefs seemed to be influenced very largely by what he had seen and read. This person read the *Daily Mail* and believed that the gun belonged to 'militant miners or a group who infiltrated miners on strike'. The BBC and ITN were described as being 'impartial and quite good' and picketing was seen as 'mostly violent apparently'. The source for this belief was given as 'TV news and newspapers'. His memories of the strike were of violence on picket lines and what had most impact on him was the 'taxi-driver being killed and bitterness'. His attitude to the police had 'not really' changed.

We can compare these answers with those of another person in the same group who read the *Sun* newspaper. This is the largest-selling paper in Britain with its well-known combination of right-wing politics, scandal, sport, and sex. It is interesting in that it is aimed at a largely working-class audience. Its readers include many people who either sympathize with or actually vote Labour. This particular reader clearly sympathized with the striking miners and it was he who wrote that television news and the newspapers were picking out violence 'so as to get a majority of people against the miners'. He thought that the BBC was 'pro-government' and that what had mostly been shown on the news was 'people trying to go to work but not able'. But in spite of believing all this, he associates the gun with striking miners. His key memories of the strike are the 'break-up of families, striking and non-striking, violence and the taxi-driver killing'. So in spite of showing a strong sympathy for the miners' cause, his beliefs and associations are actually a mixture of positive and negative elements.

Conclusions

The most obvious issue to emerge from comparing these two groups in London Transport is the difference in their attitudes towards the police. Television and press coverage of the miners' strike had affected the beliefs of people in both. But for people in the first group, their attitude toward the police and the connotations that the police had for them could act as an additional powerful influence in their interpretation of the news.

The next group of people are again from the south, but they come from one of the newer manufacturing plants situated near London.

Electronics workers – Harlow

This was a group of eleven people in an electronics factory. They came from different levels of the workforce and included managers, engineers, an inspector, and production workers. They were interviewed twenty-one months after the miners' strike had ended and produced these 'BBC news' programmes:

First BBC news

Today large crowds gathered outside Bilston Glen, consisting of miners and police, which led to an escalation of violence between riot police and the miners. At the scene later a shotgun was recovered by the police. A police spokesman later said 'violence of this nature can only lead to somebody being seriously injured or even killed'.

Talks are continuing between the NCB and the NUM officials.

Second BBC news

Following a mass meeting today of the NUM, strike action was decided.

Strike action followed immediately after discussions broke down between Scargill and MacGregor.

Angry scenes took place outside Bilston Glen where it was announced twelve more pits were to close before Christmas. Riot police had to be called in to control the crowds. Angry scuffles followed as anxious relatives watched helplessly.

Both the TUC and the police were worried by the level of violence seen today. (A senior police officer) commented at the scene that they were very anxious at the violent outbursts and at a press conference later it was announced that a weapon was found near the riots.

Third BBC news

Today the NCB announced figures on the operational pits, 25 in Scotland and 3 in Nottingham, as reported by the Chairman of the NCB Ian MacGregor.

Arthur Scargill, the president of the union at a meeting in Congress House disputed: 'The figures put out by the NCB were not true and the police are playing more than a role of peacemakers by breaking up picket lines and using unnecessary force.'

The police denied the claim and showed weapons seized at one of the picket lines.

These stories show again how some key themes are retained in the memory, such as the arguments between Arthur Scargill and Ian MacGregor over return to work figures. In the third news Scotland is presented as having more pits operational than Nottingham. In the actual history of the strike, this was not so, but these details disappear while the memory of the general argument is retained.

These stories also illustrate how a single picture can be used in different ways according to people's assumptions about the strike. In the second story above, the picture of a woman seated in a crowd of people is used as the basis for saying 'as anxious relatives watched helplessly' (Picture 7, page 16). This group contained two people who were relatively sympathetic to the miners, but as we shall see the same picture was used by other groups as evidence of what they saw as very hostile attitudes amongst the miners.

The ownership of the gun is left ambiguous by two groups. In the first there was actually a split between people who believed that it belonged to the miners. In the third group the gun is described clearly as being seized at the picket lines.

16 Electronics staff

The questions – the gun and picketing

Most people here believed that the gun belonged to the pickets/striking miners. Six thought this, two that it belonged to an outside agitator/trouble maker, two believed that it was a police weapon, and one thought that it belonged to a farmer and was unconnected to the dispute.

This group was relatively conservative in its views about television. Their attitude to the BBC was mostly that it was neutral/balanced. Six believed this while four thought that it was 'slightly biased to Conservatives/right of centre'. Two who thought this actually described themselves as 'conservative'. One person thought that the BBC was slightly biased to the left. As a group, they were not especially critical of either television or the press. Those people who had described the BBC as being slightly to the right did not link this view to criticisms of how the miners' strike had been covered.

On the issue of picketing seven of the group believed that it had in fact been mostly violent. All of these ascribed their beliefs directly to the media and most named television news as the source. Some of these replies contained the germs of criticism, but these were not followed through to a rejection of the television account. For example, one person explained her beliefs by writing that

> Most of the reports were about police/miner clashes on the picket lines. People going to work at the mines during the strike, getting beat up, etc.

But in her comments on the BBC and ITN she had written that 'both are sensationalized'. Three of the people who believed that picketing was mostly violent actually went further than this. As they answered question 6 on what had informed their view, they began to include arguments which raised doubts about their own beliefs. One commented, for example, that 'news showed mainly the violence and little peace'. He gave the reasons for his own beliefs as:

> The way they showed first, the angry clashes and emphasized them before showing the peaceful picketing and negotiations. News emphasized the violence leading us to believe there was constant violence and little peace.

A second person spoke of audience priorities saying that 'people don't want to watch two crowds of people standing around' and then went on to conclude that 'the violence aspect only lasts for a short period due to human nature, and the riot squads moving in and dispersing the crowds.' The third wrote that his beliefs about the violence came from

> continual showing of violence by television reports. Television reports, trying to show the newsworthiness of the picketing – groups of peaceful people do not usually sell news (sensationalism).

In these cases it was as if the seeds of criticism were there before the individuals were prompted to think about the issues. Their immediate response that picketing was mostly violent was then gradually undermined, as they began to explain it. As usual, everyone in this group believed that most of what they had been shown of picketing on television was violent. But four people in this group clearly rejected the television account, believing that most picketing was peaceful. One of these used logic to inform his answer, referring to the scale of the events. A second made a judgement about what human beings are like, saying that they are 'not generally violent for more than a short time'.

A longer and more complex response came from a personnel officer in the firm who referred to her own professional experience as informing her belief. She commented that 'I work with unions here all the time and they are just not violent people – they were not like that'. She also referred to the scale of the dispute and the numbers involved and in addition knew a policeman who had told her that picket duty was 'boring'. Finally, she had a sister-in-law in Nottingham who had told her that there was no violence at all there. Her views were in many ways sympathetic to the miners' side in the dispute. Her key memory of the strike was 'hardship of miners' families – breakdown of small communities'. She also believed that the police had used 'excessive force' and that they 'appeared to provoke some incidents'. This does show how complex attitudes can be, since her political views were not 'left-wing', in the sense that she read the *Daily Telegraph* and said that she actually voted Conservative.

This was a manufacturing workforce, based on a large industrial estate. Several of the group had seen or had some experience of picket lines. One person related this in a direct way to the miners' strike. This was an active trade unionist who wrote that his own experience of 'picket duty' had influenced his views of the miners' strike and police activity within it. His views were similar to those of the Yorkshire miners – he believed that picketing was peaceful and blamed 'police provocation' for any violence that occured. He quoted 'union literature' as an information source and complained specifically that the police 'waved their bulging wage-packets at the pickets, they showed no compassion or understanding'. In all, half of the group said that their attitude to the police had changed for the worse in the period since the strike. Some related this to specific events such as the strike itself and the riots in the inner cities. Others said simply that the police were now 'not good at gaining respect or trust' or that the police were now 'more hardened', and were being put in places where they had 'no right to be'. No one said that their attitude toward the police had improved. The nearest to this was a comment from a woman that the police 'can make mistakes but they get hurt too – they are forced into violence situations'. The level of negative feeling which was expressed in this group seemed surprising since political attitudes in the south are generally more conservative. But in fact the replies of the other groups showed that these were not untypical.

Memories and beliefs

The location of this group in the south and the preponderance of relatively conservative views has some important effects on these answers:

	Question 7 (**on news most**)	**Question 8** (**most personal impact**)
1	Picketing scenes	Hardship of miners' families – breakdown of small communities
2	Comments and opinions of Scargill and MacGregor	Arthur Scargill's face and windswept hair
3	Angry violent scenes outside the pits, also Arthur Scargill!	Arthur Scargill's face/innocent people getting killed (taxi-driver particularly)
4	MacGregor/breakdown of negotiations/NCB	Mr MacGregor with a paper bag over his head

5	Arthur Scargill	Nothing
6	Arthur Scargill and the violence	Violence
7	Clashes and violence between miners, police, and pickets	The killing of the occupants of the taxi when a concrete block was thrown off a bridge – how it could get so bad
8	Violence	The picket-line violence
9	The violence of the dispute, physical and verbally, i.e. Scargill v. MacGregor; miners v. police	Obstinate so-called leaders from both sides, pettiness – became a personal confrontation
10	A. Scargill	The violence of miners
11	Picketing? or union meetings, which was Scargill really/discussion programmes	Arthur Scargill

There is a form of negative fascination which Arthur Scargill apparently wields for many of the group. Over half named him as what was shown most or as what stuck most in their minds. There is also a sense of shock at the events of the strike with one person writing 'how it could get so bad'. For the active trade unionist, the key memory was Ian MacGregor 'with a paper bag over his head'. But for most of the group, the memories of Scargill, violence, and picketing seem overwhelming.

Conclusions

We have seen that what is understood and remembered can vary between groups depending on factors such as political culture and experience. But it is also clear that the media are providing a major input of information which seems to relate very directly to the beliefs of some people. Sometimes even those who were critical of the media derived important elements of what they believed and the associations that they made with the strike from media accounts.

The people interviewed in this chapter all worked outside the home. We now move to groups who are not part of the paid workforce, either because they are retired or because they are women with children.

4

Special interest groups

Activity in retirement group, Glasgow

These were elderly people who attended a regular club at a community centre in Glasgow. The news exercises were written by them one year after the end of the strike. I visited the centre for a second time shortly after this for them to complete the written questions and to speak with them further on an individual basis. Of the fourteen people here, most had been retired for several years. In the main, they had been either skilled workers or employed as secretarial/administrative staff.

Since they met regularly, they knew each other well and were familiar with each other's politics. I suggested to them that they might like to produce a variety of different types of news. Consequently, they sorted themselves very quickly into groups to produce two 'BBC news' programmes, a trade union programme and a 'Conservative' programme in the style of a documentary or news editorial.

First BBC news

Crisis in the pits.

Mr Scargill today accused the Coal Board and chiefly Mr MacGregor of holding a shot-gun to the head of the miners. The miners' case is that they want all pits to remain open and no one should lose their job. Mr Scargill says that no man should lose his job.

The Coal Board's case is that many pits are uneconomical to run and many are practically finished and millions of pounds of tax-payers' money is being wasted working these pits.

Mr MacGregor stated that no miner would lose his job as they could be transferred to new modern pits and any one not wishing to transfer could take an early retirement with substantial pay-offs.

The strike was called without a vote being taken and this was resented by miners in Nottingham and some parts of Derby.

The police had to don riot gear to stem the riots at various pits where picketing was far from legal.

(A senior police officer) reported that 18 of his men had been severely injured by men who he was quite sure were not miners but paid agitators, and that various weapons were found at the site including this shot-gun. Mr Scargill, when asked about the violence blamed the police for escalating the violence.

Second BBC news

The violence in the miners' strike has gained momentum. The police have now been issued with riot gear – the first time in British history – and among the missiles used by the miners – included a shot-gun. The chief of police is now very much concerned about the weapons being used and appeals for calm and a cooling-off period.

Arthur Scargill defends the miners' position which he says is because of antagonism by the police tactics. Ian MacGregor again calls for negotiations to take place but emphasizes the pit closures will definitely be on the agenda at any discussions.

Meantime the miners' wives generally are supporting their husbands in the cause. Now over to the miners' welfare club to get the views of their wives:

Question: What do you think of the strike?
Answer: I don't approve of the strike at all but I must support my husband.
Question: Do you approve of violence?
Answer: I definitely do not approve of violence. I think the police should have handled it better than the way they did.

Second Interviewee

Question: What do you think of the strike?
Answer: I do not approve of the strike. I don't think they benefit working people.
Question: How about violence?
Answer: I do not approve of violence.

Question: Do you find the strike is causing hardship?
Answer: Yes! It was a hardship, the family suffered.

Trade union news

As Trade Union officials we have attended various meetings and inspected various picket lines. Whilst most of the pickets were legally carried out, we must say there were disturbances at some of the lines, which we thought were due to excess authority of police who seemed to enjoy using extreme force.

The media with the help of the Government showed programmes of the picket lines in which violence occurred. One such picture of a shot-gun tended to show that a certain group had infiltrated the union and were not above using extreme violence.

We have come to the conclusion that the police as a force were used as a political weapon to break the strike.

We also feel that the Labour Party didn't give us the full backing in this strike that the Government gave to the Coal Board.

Conservative news

The first impression given by the media was the excessive violence that occurred on the picket lines. Working miners were obliged to keep weapons to safeguard their families and property, such as the one pictured.

The use of large numbers of police officers to contain the violence and the miners' leader's refusal to hold talks regarding the balloting of miners aggravated the situation.

The police are not equipped for this confrontation and should be supplied with the necessary safeguards.

The way the leaders of both sides in this dispute conducted themselves left a lot to be desired; more meetings should have been held between the two factions.

We have today with us the leader of the miners' union, Mr Arthur Scargill:

Question: Mr Scargill, what is your opinion of the police control of the picket lines?
Answer: The violence of the police on the picket lines had been deplorable. Mr MacGregor has not made a case.

The first of these news programmes offers a very competent account of some of the issues in the dispute such as the arguments over the taking of a vote for the strike. It gives details of which areas were most dissatisfied with the NUM leadership. It is also interesting in how closely it follows the Coal Board/ Government view of the dispute. The miners are represented as wishing to keep all pits open at any cost. Against this is made the case that many pits are uneconomical and that millions of pounds of tax-payers' money is being wasted in working them.

The miners' view was in fact rather different from this. During the strike, they disputed the Coal Board's figures on the economics of the industry. It was also the case that in the years before the strike the miners had accepted the closing of many pits because they were exhausted or dangerous to work. One of their concerns was that the government was deliberately running down the industry in favour of nuclear power and as a prelude to selling the most profitable sections into private ownership. The union argument was not that every pit should be kept open but rather that the government should commit itself to expansion of the industry on the lines of an agreement that had already been signed (the Plan for Coal). Whether we accept the miners' arguments or not, it is interesting how little of them have appeared in any of the news programmes that have been written by the groups.

By contrast, there is no difficulty in generating the familiar themes of 'picket-line violence', 'violence in the strike', 'escalating violence', and police 'containing violence'. The groups can also reproduce the familiar cliches of news presentation as when they introduce their own interviewees. Phrases such as 'and now over to' and 'we have with us today' are used with the ease of their own everyday vocabulary.

The first BBC group deserves some recognition for the most imaginative use of the shot-gun in their story. The Conservative group link the weapon to working miners who are presented as defending their families and property. This was very close to the context of the actual news story in which it had appeared. It is significant that two of the news stories link the gun to 'infiltrators' or 'agitators'. This turned out to be a very significant dimension in the beliefs of the group as a whole.

The questions – the gun and picketing

The fact of these people being retired was very important, since people in this age range are likely to spend a high proportion of their time at home. They are also likely to watch relatively more television than those in younger age groups. It might also be that their experience of living through the period of the second world war and its immediate aftermath had coloured their attitudes. At this time the BBC had achieved its greatest authority in its role of 'speaking for the nation'. Certainly respect for the BBC was relatively high in this group. Nine out of the fourteen people believed that it was 'balanced', 'neutral', or 'fair'. Two people believed that it was generally neutral except that it had been 'slightly biased against the miners' and three people believed that it was 'biased to the government' or 'conservative'.[1]

In the group as a whole there was a high level of belief in what they had seen on television. Ten of the group believed that most of the picketing had in reality been violent. The answers also indicate their reliance on television, with ten people giving it as their exclusive or main source of information. They regarded it as 'more visual' than newspapers and said that it was 'more immediate' and 'stuck more'. As one wrote:

> Seeing is believing.

Of those who thought that picketing was mostly peaceful, one said that it was 'made to look violent by the media'. Two said that they were in contact with ex-miners and had got their information from them. One person was unsure but said that what violence there had been was caused by 'outsiders' rather than miners. It was a very important clue to the views of the group as a whole. There were very strong feelings of sympathy expressed for the miners by six people. Amongst the others, several expressed the view that it was not miners who had caused the trouble. This view was expressed spontaneously by those who had chosen to do the 'Conservative' news. They made comments such as 'I've met a lot of miners' and 'a better crowd you couldn't get'. Not everyone felt like this and there was some criticism expressed especially of the miners' leaders. But overall, miners as a body of people were not seen as being violent. There was obviously some contradiction between this feeling and the trust that most of the group were putting in the images from television. This was resolved by blaming the trouble on outside elements such as the 'infiltrators' and 'paid agitators'. These views came out most strongly in their answers on the ownership of the gun, with eight people including the words 'agitator', 'activist' or 'militant' in their answer. One other person said that he didn't associate the gun with the strike but that any trouble had been was caused by 'agitators'. Of the remaining people, two associated the gun with the police and three with striking miners/pickets.

Memories and beliefs

Whatever they thought about the miners as people, the group was certainly not united in their attitude to the strike. The divisions of opinion are shown clearly in these memories:

	Question 7 (**on news most**)	**Question 8** (**most personal impact**)
1	Not known	Closing of mines
2	Conflict miners and police	Police galloping down at people/miners breaking away (to form new union)
3	Picketing or Scargill shouting the odds	Stupidity of people
4	Scargill/militants	Violence
5	Fighting and union leaders	Fighting between miners and police
6	Picket lines, violence, police activity	Picket lines at various places
7	Violence and fighting between miners and police	What the police had to put up with and the arrogance of McGahey and Scargill
8	The violence of the picket lines	Mr Scargill's unflappability when under pressure from the opposition – he was never without an answer
9	Militants, Arthur Scargill etc.	The women backing the miners after seeing so much picket-line violence
10	Police in attendance	Police being involved in the violence

11	Miners in the wrong all the time	Fear of loss of mines and work
12	Arthur Scargill	Attitudes of police (causing trouble)
13	Violent confrontations between miners and police	Lack of provision for peaceful picketing (legal picketing prevented by police). Government so-called lack of interference – yet millions spent on oil to keep industries going
14	Fighting, violence between police and pickets	Violence

These do show that the criticism of Arthur Scargill is not confined to the south of the country. But there is perhaps not the level of hostility here that existed in some of the southern groups. There are some very subtle nuances in the attitudes expressed. For example, the respondent who is numbered 8 in the list is not especially sympathetic to the strike. His attitude to the police was that 'they do a grand job under the most trying and dangerous situations'. Yet he can still comment in a wry fashion on Mr Scargill's 'unflappability'. The second respondent above is clearly very unsympathetic to the miners' leader and writes of 'Scargill shouting the odds'. But the attitudes seem to be coloured by a form of weary familiarity rather than a sense of moral outrage.

Once again there are many references to violence in the strike. The replies also show the sharp divisions of opinion within the group over the role of the police. These vary from concern over 'what the police had to put up with' to comments on 'police being involved in the violence'. In the direct question on attitudes to the police, five people expressed positive views saying for example that they were 'in favour of law and order' and commenting that the police 'have a difficult job'. For two there was no change and seven said that their views were now more negative. One of these commented that 'the police were okay, the government made them act the way they did in the strike'. This link was made by others saying, for example, that 'the police were being used politically as a military force' and that the police were 'aligned with the National Coal Board and Mr MacGregor'.

The replies also provided more evidence of how personal history and experience could affect perceptions of the strike. One woman commented that she believed 'the police were causing the trouble'. She based this view on her own experience of living in Easterhouse, a large working-class housing estate on the outskirts of the city. There, she said, the police 'had been awful hard on the boys'. This was not a recent experience, since it was twenty years since she had lived there, but it still conditioned her interpretations of what she saw on television. At the same time, she and many others in the group were worried about the problem of 'law and order'. This was perhaps intensified for them because of their age and vulnerability. As the woman from Easterhouse commented 'the police change, but we still need them'.

Conclusions

This group is notable for its high reliance on television news as a source of information. Two-thirds of the people believed that most picketing that had taken place was violent. Some of these were clearly sympathetic to the striking miners and there was sadness expressed at how the violence reflected on the miners' cause. But because of the level of sympathy which existed in the group, there was a strong tendency to link the source of the trouble to 'outside' elements. Some people also blamed the police for being involved in the violence. But what is interesting about the beliefs on 'agitators, infiltrators, and militants' is that they were held by people who differed in their views on the role of the police and in their support of the strike. What they shared was a common belief that if the strike was violent then miners as a body were not likely to have acted in this way. Of course there are other influences on beliefs about militants and agitators. Some of the group read right-wing newspapers such as the *Daily Express*, for whom 'militants' are a favourite target. The vocabulary of 'who was to be blamed' was generally available. Indeed, we have seen how individuals in other groups have used the same explanation. The issue is why so many in this group used it. Perhaps the key to understanding their response is that they were essentially rooted in the 'respectable' political traditions of skilled workers and the lower middle classes. It is perhaps this combination of the belief in an 'acceptable' politics and trade unionism, plus sympathy for the miners, that leads so many to choose the agitators/militants theory to explain what they have seen and believed on the news.[2]

We turn now to three more groups of people who are not employed outside the home. They are all women, most of whom had young children.

Women in community centres – Glasgow

These interviews were at community centres in the Gorbals/ Hutcheson and Milton areas of Glasgow which are working-class parts of the city. Most of the women attended the centres to take advantage of nursery facilities to which they brought their children. They also took part in informal discussion groups which were arranged with some help from the local authority and a local association for adult education.[3]

The meetings were held between ten months and one year after the strike ended. They were originally part of the pilot stages of the study while the final methodology was still being developed. The news writing exercise was conducted in the usual way. But the second half of the meeting took the form of a general discussion of the questions, and a record was kept of the replies to specific ones, such as the ownership of the gun and key memories of the strike. Since these provided very important points of comparison with the groups in the South, I decided to include them here.

The women were interviewed in two separate groups of four and six people. Between them they produced two 'BBC' news programmes and one trade union/Channel 4 style news:

First group – BBC news

> The introduction of Mr Ian MacGregor as Chairman of the National Coal Board, in a government effort to streamline and make the coal industry economically productive was opposed by the NUM and their President, Arthur Scargill. The strike led to divided loyalties between families, unions, and the eventual formation of a breakaway union in Nottingham.
>
> Mass picketing resulted in the police force being severely criticized for their deployment of military-type crowd control. Riot gear became a common sight on the picket line.

To support the miners, who were not in receipt of strike pay, fund-raising events were organized. Soup kitchens opened and the women of the communities became a support system for their men.

The discovery of a shot-gun by police presents a new element in the control of picketing.

Second group – BBC news

Today Ian MacGregor condemned the action at Bilston Glen colliery of the miners in the picket line in the continuing battle between the miners and the police.

It is reported that a gun was fired at the police and although no actual injuries occurred, the police chief in charge of the riot police commented that this was a very serious matter and could lead to the police being armed in the future with riot shields and plastic bullets.

In the studio tonight we have Inspector (X).

Question: Inspector, what is your reaction to the incident of the shot-gun today?

Answer: I feel that once weapons are introduced into this matter, it is time for the government to introduce the appropriate legislation to allow the police in this country to carry weapons – in order to defend themselves, as the police in other countries are allowed to do.

Arthur Scargill speaking from Congress House denied all knowledge of the affair and refused to comment further.

Second group – trade union/Channel 4 news

Tonight on the 10th month of the miners' strike reports are coming in of mass pickets at the Bilston Glen colliery where according to NCB reports 12 men are reported to have returned to work. The police were yet again seen to be fully armed with riot shields and batons at the ready, yet again inciting an already angry crowd, who are, in this country of free speech, after all only fighting for their jobs and their future, that Mr MacGregor is determined to destroy.

Meanwhile earlier on today Arthur Scargill visited Kiverton colliery down south, where a mass rally was taking place with miners from all over Yorkshire. Wives, children, and all were

> seen to be there. Among the crowds we spoke to many miners' wives, all totally committed to the strike and willing to face any hardships incurred by it.
>
> The Chief Inspector of the Metropolitan police today reported the discovery of a double-barrelled shot-gun at the Kiverton colliery, concealed between two stone walls at a shaft entrance. Once again he states this is the reason his men have to be protected while carrying out their duties. Once again is this a cover story for the police tactics seen time and time again over the months?

These women were mostly working-class in their background and expressed a strong sympathy for the miners' cause. I asked the first group what they would have included in their news if they had been writing a trade union version. They replied 'that the government was trying to break the strike'. But even though they are critical, they seem to have absorbed the government and Coal Board's description of what the dispute is about. The appointment of Ian MacGregor is seen as being simply to 'streamline and make the coal industry economically productive'.

We see again the familiar themes of 'mass pickets', 'angry crowds', and the 'return to work'. They also contained an additional emphasis on 'police tactics', 'riot gear', and 'arming the police'. The role of the police in the strike was important in these groups and some of their beliefs are shown in the manner in which the shot-gun is included in their report. The trade union group suggest openly that it is a 'cover story' to justify police tactics. One presents it as being fired at the police without saying who is responsible. The first group seem unsure how to use it and put a sentence in at the end saying that it has been discovered and that it presents new questions in the control of picketing.

Both groups were asked: Who did the gun belong to? Two thought that it was planted by the police, two others that it was 'planted' or 'planted by someone to cause trouble'. One person didn't connect it to the strike. Five thought that it belonged to pickets or striking miners. One of these in the second group actually justified them having a gun in the circumstances as they were 'fighting for a just cause'. This led to much dissent and a consensus was established that it was not reasonable to use guns as 'innocents might be hurt'.

In their support for the miners, the women in both groups were very close to the views of the Scottish trade unionists. About the same proportion believed that the gun had been 'planted'. They differed in that the women were much more reliant on television as a source of information than were the trade unionists. Although the father of one of the women had been a miner, none spoke of any direct contact with the strike or anyone involved. Some did note the special impact of television, saying that 'it shows it live'. A majority of the women believed that most picketing in the strike had involved violence and fighting. Less than one in five had believed this amongst the trade unionists. Television was blamed by some for distorting the violence. One commented that 'the camera would only pick on what will be news'. Most of them actually believed that television news was 'pro-government' or 'biased against the miners'. This had not stopped many of them from accepting the images of fighting as being typical. But there was a strong association of violence with the police. One commented that 'police are [now] given more licence to be violent' and another that since the strike the police were 'more pushy – police violence was [now] more acceptable'. These views on the police had clearly affected some memories of the strike. One commented that what she thought was shown most on television was 'police holding back picketing miners, causing aggression'.

There is another comparison which we can make here between the Glasgow women and the Activity in retirement group. Most of the retired people had believed that television news was neutral and impartial. The news which they saw had mostly attributed violence to the miners/pickets. This is perhaps one reason why so many of them blamed 'agitators, infiltrators, and militants' for the trouble. But in the group of women, most did not believe that television was impartial. As one commented 'they only showed violence from miners, not police'. It is possible to take from television the belief that picketing was mostly violent, but to reject its account of the cause. In such a scenario, there is no special reason to blame agitators.

All of the Glasgow women believed that most of what television had shown of picketing was violent. In the second group, a woman offered a reason for this, saying: 'they need to show you that or you would just carry on with what you were doing in the house'. It was clearly no surprise to these people that the television is left on while many other activities are in progress. But although this woman acknowledged the eye-catching nature of violent images, these were not in fact the ones which she remembered most clearly from the strike. When this group was asked what stuck most in their minds, she immediately said that it was people 'queueing for food – I thought, the poor souls'. Two other women in this group also gave this as a key memory. This list of memories is in the order in which they were generated by the group:

1 Queueing for food
2 Anger at miners complaining [on television and in the press] that they didn't get messages [shopping and food] if they weren't on the picket lines – they shouldn't just sit at home on their arses
3 Miner grabbing MacGregor [when he fell through a fence]
4 Arthur Scargill getting too hysterical on television and losing his case

These were from my first meeting with this group. I returned at a later date for further discussion with them. They then added some other memories which included again a reference to 'Arthur Scargill making a mess of the whole miners' case'. There were also several more references to 'queueing for food', 'collecting money', and 'begging for money to feed their families'. One person also added 'endless futile discussions' and 'miner killed by picketing miners'. This last event did not in fact happen so it is perhaps a reference to the death of the Welsh taxi-driver. There was also one mention of 'splitting families up i.e. father and son on different sides'.

The first group also gave their list of key memories which are given here in the order in which they were generated:

1 Violence
2 Horses galloping
3 Size of crowds
4 People hungry
5 Wonderful how people stuck together/sight of people sharing together, sitting in clubs, the women preparing food
6 And the other side of it – the bitterness and divisions within the community, families split

These memories again show the sympathies of the women for

the strike and also say something of their own position and the difficulties of their own lives. There was an immediate identification by several of the group with 'queueing for food', 'people hungry', and 'collecting money'. The role of the women in the strike and people standing together are spoken of very positively in their news stories.

There is also a sadness mentioned by two people at the divisions and bitterness caused by the strike. But there is no shock expressed at the intensity of such feelings within the mining communities.

Their view of Arthur Scargill is also significant as 'messing up the miners' case'. Some, in other groups felt the same. One of the senior partners in the Glasgow solicitors' office had commented that 'Scargill tended to alienate people like me who would have been sympathetic'. But what is most interesting about the women's observation is that it shows the detachment with which they can view Scargill's television performance. Their sympathies for the strike did not overwhelm their judgement. They could in a sense stand back and evaluate his performance as it would be received by others.

These women were notable for their very strong commitment to the miners cause. We go now to the south-east of the country, to a group of women in Bromley, Kent.

Mothers' and toddlers' group, Bromley, Kent

Bromley is a very middle-class suburb of London. It features miles of detached houses and elects a Conservative MP and local council. Culturally and politically it is a long way from Glasgow.

This group of women all had young children. Most had originally met because their maternity hospital had a policy of bringing new mothers together to give mutual support. This one had largely sustained itself and now, with three other women from the area, met as an informal mothers' and toddlers' group. This meeting was in the extensive home of one of the women. Before they had children, three of the group had worked as teachers; there was also a solicitor, an advertising executive, a personnel assistant, a social worker, and two nurses.

Writing the news

It was fourteen months since the strike had ended. When I explained the exercise, there was some concern expressed that they might not be able to remember anything about it. One of the women picked up a picture of Ian MacGregor and said, 'Oh, is that a Coal Board official?' She then said, 'That shows how much television we watched. We used to turn it off, it was so boring.' Another woman said, 'Yes, so did we.' Then, the sight of the pictures apparently had the usual effect of triggering a large number of memories and associations. After the exercise was completed, the first of the two women came back to me and said:

> When you first asked me, I said I never watched it – then when you asked the questions I found it was amazing how much I remembered – how much you take in.

The women were already familiar with each other and sorted themselves into a trade union and a 'BBC news' group. Since this division seemed to represent clear differences of opinion, I asked them to explain their preferences. Most in the BBC group wrote that they preferred it because they 'did not agree with' trade unions or 'did not sympathize with or support' the trade union view. Most of the women in the trade union group wrote that they did sympathize with the miners cause. These are the news stories which they produced.

Trade union news

> Police brutality continues in Kent coalfields.
>
> Police outnumbered miners two to one. Many scuffles broke out, more than 150 miners arrested, 50 suffering injuries.
>
> Miners' leader, Arthur Scargill, addressing miners later in the day at a rally for miners and their wives, said: 'This is a sad day for the trade union movement when a trade unionist can no longer peacefully picket without harrassment from the police.'
>
> Meanwhile police in Nottinghamshire are making extensive enquiries regarding a shot-gun discovered in the home of a working miner. It is believed to be the same gun used in an earlier incident in which striking miners were threatened on their way to the welfare club.

(A senior police officer) made no comment.

BBC news

Good evening. This is the BBC news. Figures released from the Coal Board this evening show return to work at Bilston Glen and Kiverton Park.

At both collieries there was massive picketing to prevent an increase in this trend. Joining the picket lines are many wives supporting their husbands.

At Bilston Glen scuffles broke out with police and 35 pickets were arrested.

(A senior police officer) in charge of police operations reported the finding of several missiles and a shot-gun. He fears that violence is escalating and he is concerned for the safety of his officers.

Ian MacGregor – Coal Board chief, commented that miners should not be prevented from returning to work and he is totally opposed to victimization of working miners.

Arthur Scargill questioned police tactics and suggested the shot-gun had been planted.

Both of these news programmes give accounts of the conflict on the picket lines. The first has been clearly influenced by the views of one of the group whose brother is a journalist. He had written on events in Nottinghamshire where a majority of the miners did not take part in the strike. This was the prelude to a deep split in the miners union and the formation of a breakaway union (the Union of Democratic Mineworkers). The access which this group had to such detailed knowledge has resulted in the gun being put in the hands of a working miner and being used to threaten those on strike.

The second news offers a very different view in which the 'victimization' is being done by the striking miners. This news is also interesting for the range of themes which it covers. It gives the names of two coalpits, but there is no significance in this as they are indicated in the photographs that are being used. But it is significant that the group should identify them as relating to the familiar themes of escalating violence, mass picketing, scuffles, and arrests. As with the last group, the role of women in the strike is also featured. The last line of their news carries the firm suggestion, attributed to Arthur Scargill, that the shot-gun has been planted. But this account of the gun was not in fact given by any of the women in the statements that they made about their own beliefs.

The questions – the gun and picketing

All five of the women in the BBC group believed that the gun belonged to striking miners/pickets. Of the four people in the trade union group, two wrote that they did not connect the gun with the dispute. A third woman who was very sympathetic to the miners actually wrote the words 'striking miner'. She then apparently realized the possible contradiction between this and her own sympathies. She crossed out what she had written and put 'don't know'. The fourth person wrote simply that the gun belonged to a 'striking miner'. She was in fact more ambivalent in her attitude to the miners' cause.

These are important examples because they show that the placing of the gun does 'work' in some way to illustrate how our sympathies and beliefs affect the associations that we make. They also show how these sympathies can sometimes be overlaid in a contradictory way with other connotations which may be made for us in the media. The exercise itself could act as a stimulus to resolve such contradictions. A further example of this came when a woman in the trade union group wrote that she believed picketing was mostly violent. She gave as her source for this 'the TV news'. But when she expressed her view in the discussion, she was immediately challenged by another woman from the trade union group, whereupon she revised her view and said that she could see that picketing probably wasn't mostly violent, because of things she had read in the *Guardian* and had already thought about. Yet somehow, as she said, the impression had remained with her that picketing *was* mostly violent. But it was not until it was discussed in the group that the contradictions between what she had read and what she had seen on television were resolved. This was an interesting case since she, along with most of the group, had already expressed doubts about the impartiality of television news, saying of the BBC that it was 'establishment'. She had also chosen the trade union group because as she wrote 'I sympathized with trade unions' and she had in fact been involved in union actions herself as a teacher.

In the group as a whole five out of the nine people wrote that they believed picketing to be mostly violent. They gave as their source 'television news', 'the media', 'newspapers and television' and two people also mentioned radio along with TV news. This reliance on the media was summarized by one of the women in the comment:

> My opinion of the miners' strike was totally influenced by the media, both press and TV, since I have no first-hand knowledge of the strike and conditions, nor do I know anyone with first-hand knowledge.

None of the women had any direct experience of the strike or had been on a picket line. Of those who rejected the television account of picketing, two had compared it with information from other sources such as the quality press, television documentaries or 'alternative' local radio. One had the brother who was a journalist and had taken her information from him. Lastly, one of the women who had been in the BBC group and who had rather conservative views, cast doubt on the reliability of television as a medium. She wrote that she was unsure about picketing because 'was television only showing violence since peaceful picketing is not interesting news?' This view of television is sometimes thought of as 'common knowledge'. But it was not applied by most of this group to their understanding of the strike.

Memories and beliefs

These show some of the differences between the women in their attitudes to the dispute. But perhaps more interestingly they also show what they hold in common:

	Question 7 (**on news most**)	**Question 8** (**most personal impact**)
1	Picketing and victimizing working miners	Scargill – because he's biased and attention-seeking
2	Violence – police – Arthur Scargill	Violence, taxi-driver death
3	Picket lines, Ian MacGregor and Arthur Scargill	People arguing, picket lines

4	Picket lines	Picket lines, violence
5	Picket lines	Police v. miners confrontation
6	Violence against police by miners and harrassment of working miners by striking miners	Picket line, violence
7	Violence on the picket line	Police tactics
8	Picketing and discussions or lack of, between NCB and NUM	Arthur Scargill's stubborness and the formation of the breakaway miners' union (Notts. miners)
9	Violence on the picket lines, and Arthur Scargill	Injured miners and policemen

Once again picket lines and violence came very high in people's memories. This to some extent cuts across differences in political attitudes. In the above list the respondent numbered 1 is not at all sympathetic with the miners' cause, while the respondent numbered 6 had the opposite attitude and is extremely sympathetic. Yet both believe that what was most shown on the news was 'victimization' and 'harrassment' of working miners. The differences in attitudes between the women become more apparent in their memories of what had most personal impact upon them. Some make specific criticisms of Arthur Scargill, while another mentions 'police tactics'. This memory of the police in the strike had in fact been conditioned by personal experience. The woman wrote that her view of violence in the strike had been influenced by 'personal knowledge of incidents involving the police'. She wrote as follows:

> I was a victim of an April Fool's joke by half a dozen policemen who stopped me in my car one night saying that a car fitting the description of mine had been spotted at the scene of a robbery. They turfed everything out of my car on to the pavement and when nothing was found announced that it was just after midnight on April 1st. They all laughed and got in their cars and drove off.

In all, four of the nine women said that their attitudes to police had changed for the worse in the period since the strike, while the remaining five said there was no change in their attitude. There were certainly strong differences between these women in their attitude to the strike and to the police. Yet many of them shared the same memories of violence and the events of the picket lines, albeit that there were differences in who they thought was responsible for the trouble.

There is a sharp contrast to be drawn between this group as a whole and the women in Glasgow. No one in the Bromley group, whatever their sympathies, had 'people going hungry', 'queueing for food', or 'loss of money' as what had stuck most in their minds. This is perhaps an example of perception being shaped by class experience, which in this case is distinct from political sympathy. Some of the Bromley women had the same sympathies as those of the Glasgow women. There was also something shared between both groups in their presentation of the role of women in the strike. But only one of them was close to the experience of real deprivation.

Political culture and class experience can combine in certain ways to influence perception and memory. We can explore this further by comparing the views of the last two groups with those of working-class women in the south. We go now to a group of mothers in Penge, in south London.

Penge community playgroup, south London

This was a group of women who attended a mothers' and toddlers' group in a hall which was loaned to them by a local church. Penge is a predominantly working-class area, but has few nursery facilities provided by the local authority. In all, eight women completed the exercise and the questions. It was fourteen months since the strike had ended.

The women themselves were from the local area and most had worked in shops, hospital cleaning, or as clerical staff. They expressed no preference for any particular news group and agreed simply to do 'the news'. This lack of distinction between programmes was significant. It reflected a shared belief that 'they all distort the truth' or 'all lie', which four people wrote of both BBC and ITV. Two others thought that both channels were 'pro-establishment' and the remaining two believed that they 'just reported the facts'. Here are their programmes:

17 Mothers' and toddlers' group, Penge

First television news

Today it has been reported that a gun was found at Kiverton Park where three miners returned to work. More police were called in as the miners' tempers flared. (A senior police officer) reported today that various firearms and weapons were being used.

Ian MacGregor and Arthur Scargill attended another meeting at Congress House which finished abruptly with more arguments and no decision reached.

Second television news

There were reports today that a shot-gun was found at the home of a working miner. The police were seriously disturbed by this incident.

The Chairman of the Coal Board said he was not surprised at this news, as it showed the fear that working miners are living under.

Mr Scargill said that this shows that violence was prevalent throughout the industry and showed the lengths to which the government has driven the ordinary working person.

The first of these highlights the now familiar theme of the return to work, tempers flaring, meetings, and arguments. The second news concentrates on the story of the gun. There were divisions between the women over this. The person who suggested that it should be given in the story to a working miner was very opposed to the strike. She said 'If I was a working miner, I'd have shot them all, an' all'. But others were more sympathetic and there was a comment included on the 'length to which the government has driven the ordinary working person'.

The questions – the gun and picketing

Their beliefs about the gun were mostly that it belonged to striking miners or a picket. Six believed this and one other said that it belonged to 'a violent person' – of no particular side.

Two believed that it belonged to the police. One of these was able to answer only this question, as she had to leave to attend to her child. Her reply was interesting since her husband had been involved in the picketing at Wapping (in the print dispute) and he had been injured while there. Her opinion of the police had changed for the worse, and this was perhaps a factor in her association of them with the gun.

On the issue of picketing, the group were evenly split. The four who believed that it was mostly violent all cited television as their source. Two also mentioned newspapers and one included radio. One of these cases was interesting since the woman had been confined to her bed for most of the strike. The information on the strike was conveyed to her by her husband straight from the television.

Of those who rejected the television account, one was in the Labour Party and had spoken with miners, and one other said simply that 'television exaggerates a lot'. Another employed the value commitment which we have already seen, that most people are not violent. She commented that:

> I think there was a lot they didn't show and I thought this was mostly peaceful – it was just thinking the best of people I suppose.

Finally, one person referred to the number of people on strike as her reason for disbelieving television. This was an important example, since this was the woman who had earlier said that she would have shot striking miners. Yet she used the following argument to reject the television account of violence:

> Television just shows the violent bits. They won't show people just standing around. [It was mostly peaceful] because of the amount who were actually on strike, if you take that into account, it can't all have been violent.

It is important to note that such a critique of television and the use of logical processes can cut across personal and political sympathies.

Memories and beliefs

Once again picketing and violence predominate, but these memories also show something of the different strands of opinion within the group:

	Question 7 (on news most)	**Question 8 (most personal impact)**
1	The violent clashes between miners and police	The destruction of friendships
2	Violence on picket lines, and number of miners returning to work	History, long dispute, the cost
3	Picket lines	People all out of work
4	Picket lines	People out of work
5	Meetings and picket lines	Long dispute
6	Picketing	Arthur Scargill
7	Attacks on miners' homes and police clashes with pickets	Arthur Scargill and picket lines
8	The picket lines and confrontations between police and miners	Picket lines and Arthur Scargill

There is not the intense level of sympathy shown here which we found in some working-class groups in Scotland. The Labour Party member believes that 'the numbers of miners returning to work' was shown most on the news. But as a whole the group is divided in its attitudes to the strike and some of the women indicate a personal ambivalence over the issues involved. For example, the woman who said that she would shoot the striking miners puts as her key memory of the strike 'the destruction of friendships'. There is a current of sympathy within the group which is not overtly political. There are no memories which involve criticism of government or police action, but two of the women write: 'people out of work'. Unemployment is close to them as a class experience, and in this their replies differ from those of the women in Bromley.

On their attitudes to the police, two of the women did make possible links between these and their perception of the strike. The woman whose husband was injured at Wapping and the Labour Party member had both believed that the gun belonged to the police. The second of these also wrote that since the strike it was 'now clearer that they support the establishment'. Two other women also expressed negative views of the police, four said there was no change in their attitude and one said that she now found the police 'more friendly, helpful, and approachable'.

Conclusions

This group expressed a high level of distruct in media. Yet it was clear that the beliefs of several of the women were very much influenced by what they had seen in the news.

It was also clear, in looking at the three groups of women as a whole, that what was finally believed and remembered was influenced by a range of political, class, and cultural variables. The political culture of the Glasgow women showed in their strong support for the miners and in the criticism made of television's account of the origins of violence. The women in Bromley were more divided but some shared these sympathies. The role of the police was also raised as an issue within their group. The Penge women were again divided, showing less sympathy than those in Glasgow for the miners. But there was a dimension of class experience which linked the women in Penge and Glasgow. Both groups raised the issue of deprivation caused by the strike. But in Bromley, no one had 'being out of work' or 'queueing for food' as their key memories of the events.

Within these groups we have also seen both criticism of television as a medium and the use of logical processes to evaluate coverage. We have the example of a middle-class woman in Bromley who was sympathetic to the striking miners, yet who accepted the television images of violence. By contrast, a woman from Penge who was unsympathetic offered a coherent critique of what television news had shown. It appears that such processes are not necessarily tied to class or political sympathies.

We now move on to interviews with residential groups. The samples of people in this study as a whole are relatively small. They were chosen to illustrate possible differences of perception rather than to be representative of the total population. It was useful to broaden the sample with further groups from the south of the country, since such a large section of the population is located there. In the event they provided some very important points of comparison.

5

Residential groups

These groups were assembled by bringing people together who lived in a specific street or block of flats in a given area. The interviews took place in the home of one of the local residents. This person was usually known to me and was not included in the sample. In each case I asked him/her to invite all the immediate neighbours to take part, irrespective of whether they were actually known to them or not. This procedure was useful in that it held constant the areas in which the group lived and the type/size of their home. I could then check in the individual interviews on other possible differences within the group, for example, of occupation, class background, or experience.

Bromley residents

This area was a little less expensive than the part of Bromley visited earlier and the house in which we met was more modest. Several of this group had lived in their present homes for many years and had purchased them for very much less than their present market value. This had been greatly inflated in recent years by the boom in property prices in the south-east.

There were nine people in the group and they were interviewed fourteen months after the strike. Most were in their late middle age or were now retired. Some were from skilled working-class backgrounds including a building trade foreman, two print workers, and a watch-maker/technician; while others in the group gave their occupations as a director of an advertising agency and a company representative. Two women in the group described themselves as housewives and one other as a clerk/secretary/housewife.

There were no preferences expressed to write either a 'BBC' or a trade union news, though as it turned out there were very strong differences of opinion within the group. Two people who eventually worked on the 'BBC news' said that they had watched very little of the strike because of their attitude to Arthur Scargill. 'As soon as he came on we switched off,' they said. Consequently, I told them what some of the pictures represented as I wished them to take part and was interested in how they would place the gun.[1] As it turned out they, along with all the others, had their own key memories of the strike. Here are their news programmes:

BBC news

Today at Congress House there was a meeting between the TUC and the NUM. On leaving the meeting Mr Scargill said, to waiting reporters, that he would be reporting back to his executive committee but he was sure that the strike would continue as no suitable offer had been made.

Mr MacGregor, chairman of the Coal Board, reported that thirteen men had returned to work at the Bilston Glen colliery and three at Kiverton Park and he was sure that more men would be following suit.

Police were out in force, some in riot gear trying to combat picket violence. The Chief Constable stated that a double-barrelled shot-gun had been found.

At the miners clubs, fundraising concerts had been held and miners' wives had got together to provide meals for the families.

Trade union news

After a meeting at Congress House today with the TUC executive, Arthur Scargill issued a statement protesting against allegations by the police that pickets were using firearms to dissuade fellow miners from returning to work at Kiverton Park colliery, where only three started on the early morning shift today out of a total of 246 on strike.

Miners all over the country are receiving food parcels and cash received from various fundraising activities, and other trade unions at home and abroad. This will help them to continue in their struggle against Mr MacGregor and his threat to close uneconomic pits.

Since I had explained some of the pictures, there is less significance in the direct references to them, such as the comments on 'fundraising' and the return to work figures. Some information which the group used was also contained in the pictures, such as the names of collieries. But it is interesting that the group generated from their own resources so many themes which did not relate directly to the photos at all. We see again a reference to 'uneconomic pits' and to miners' wives providing 'meals for the families'. There is also a reference to 'food parcels' and to help from 'other trade unions at home and abroad'; and to the difficulties in negotiations with 'no suitable offer' being made.

In both stories, the gun is associated by implication with strikers/pickets in the dispute, though in the trade union news Arthur Scargill is actually denying that it has been used to 'dissuade' miners from returning to work.

The questions – the gun and picketing

The issue of who owns the gun produced some sharply contrasting views. Four people associated it with 'striking miners/pickets' and one thought that it belonged to an 'agitator'. Two associated it with the police and two did not connect it with anyone in the dispute. But there were some interesting qualifications made to the beliefs. One of those who thought it belonged to the police said that they were 'carrying it for their own protection'. By contrast the other wrote that the police had it 'to discredit the pickets'. Meanwhile one of those who thought that it belonged to a picket wrote that its purpose was 'to discredit the police'. We thus had the idea of it being used as a 'plant' by both sides in the dispute. The reference to the agitator was also important. It came from one of the print workers who wrote that the gun belonged to 'somebody on picket lines – not necessarily a union man, an agitator'. We see here again the distinction between legitimate union people and 'outsiders'.

Some of this group had very pronounced conservative views. No one thought that the BBC was 'right-wing'. Most believed it to be 'very fair', 'unbiased', 'middle-of-the-road', or 'balanced'. Six people believed this while two thought that it was 'leftist' or 'left of centre'. One thought that it was 'middle-of-road/slightly left-wing?' This group also produced some remarkable division of opinion over the nature of picketing. Four people believed that most of what had taken place was violent – some making their point very emphatically. One added, for example, that 'most of the picketing was unlawful!'. But one of the print workers was more ambivalent, writing that it was 'mostly violent, but some areas very quiet'. The second print worker rejected the view completely, writing that it was 'on the whole probably peaceful'. He then added that:

> Having been in the trade, I don't believe the journalists. TV and newspaper journalists, they're all the same breed.

Of the others who rejected the news account, one knew people who had been at the picket lines and also spoke of comparing reports in the quality press with those on television. One of the women wrote of the scale of the strike, noting that it was not mostly violent because 'otherwise there would be a revolution if there was violence everywhere'. She was not herself committed to the overthrow of the established order. In fact, in reply to the question on which newspaper she preferred she commented 'anything nice with the royal family in it'.

Two other people in this group believed that picketing was mostly peaceful. These were the retired director of the advertising agency and his wife. At first sight their views were something of a puzzle. In most respects their replies were fairly conservative. Their key memories of the strike were: 'Mr Scargill talking rubbish/lies' and they both believed that the police 'do a wonderful job and always have'. The BBC was seen by them as being 'very fair/unbiased'. At the same time they believed that most of what television had shown of picketing was violent. Yet they both clearly rejected this view of picketing. I asked them their reasons for this and they mentioned possible differences between what they had read in the papers and had seen on television. The papers which they took were the *Daily Mail* and the *Sunday Express* and I asked if they thought there was a marked difference between the account given in these and what they had seen on television. The husband then said:

> Also, we stayed in the village of Ollerton, a wonderful place; that was where the picket was killed, and knowing the people there and the wonderful – there was a carvery restaurant there and all the miners and their children used to come in, wonderful people – and that influenced my opinion.

His wife then commented: 'Every time it came on we were looking for Ollerton'. This is an important example because it shows the contradictions which experience can build in to our perception. There is an uneasy tension in their views, for example, between the belief that television is very fair and impartial and their rejection of its presentation of picketing. At the same time their view of the miners as wonderful people co-exists with one of them writing that the shot-gun belonged to a striking miner, and the other that it was being carried by the police for their own protection.

Memories and beliefs

Some of the different sympathies within the group are highlighted here:

	Question 7 (on news most)	Question 8 (most personal contact)
1	Violence	Mr Scargill talking rubbish
2	Violence	Arthur Scargill's lies
3	Picketing by the mob!	Not a good thought for the miners/waste
4	The hardship to the miners and cold weather	Utter waste of time and effort on the part of the miners
5	Violent crowds and shouting and hardship of wives and kids	Mr MacGregor being knocked over
6	Picketing and hardship for the families, food parcels	The view of the taxi after the stone had dropped from the bridge
7	Don't remember, apart from various groups coming out of meetings	The tragedy of splits in families where some worked during the strike
8	Violence on picket lines	Hate between working and striking miners
9	Don't remember	Mr Scargill/police being attacked from all sides while trying to do a difficult job/also hate between miners

Some of the most sympathetic references to the miners, for example, to the hardships of their families, come from the respondents numbered 4, 5, and 6. These are one of the print workers, the watch-maker/technician, and the building trade foreman. Those numbered 1, 2, and 3 are the ex-advertising director, his wife, and the company representative. For the first of these, their feelings about Arthur Scargill have clearly overwhelmed other memories. None of this group were close to economic hardships themselves, though most would perhaps have had some contact with deprivation because of their age and the experience of living through the war. But it is interesting that only the skilled workers identify with the hardship of the strike, which perhaps again says something of the relation between class experience and perception.

The respondent numbered 9 offers a very positive memory of the police, describing them as 'being attacked from all sides while trying to do a difficult job'. This was from the wife of the second print worker. He was now·retired and had left the printing trade about five years before these interviews took place. His attitude to the police had improved:

> Because of the way they handled the miners' strike under extreme provocation and handled it well in the circumstances.

By contrast the other print worker, who was still employed, wrote of 'police brutality'. In all, eleven print workers were interviewed for this study. The retired printer was the only one whose opinion had improved. He had left the printing trade before most of the controversy over new technology and the events of Wapping. It is not possible to say what his views would have been had he stayed longer but it is interesting that he was the only one amongst all the print workers who felt as he did.

Amongst the Bromley residents, five wrote favourably of the police; one said there was no change in attitude; and three wrote that their attitude had changed for the worse in the period since the miners strike. The negative comments included saying that the police are being 'used politically' and are 'more aggressive'. The positive comments included a reference to the number of criticisms that had recently been made of the police. The respondent numbered 9 above wrote that she had 'sympathy for the police with so many people denigrating them'. This was said in the context of several news stories which were running in this period about the police. Labour MPs had that evening called for an enquiry into the role of the police in the Wapping print dispute.

These interviews with groups of residents made it possible to compare the evaluations of television coverage made by people who lived in the same family unit. There were three married couples in the above group. In the event, the building trade foreman and his wife (numbers 6 and 7 above) did agree on their rejection of television's portrayal of violence. But the ex-print worker and his wife (numbers 8 and 9) differed since he referred to his experience 'in the trade' to inform his criticism of journalists. The third couple, the ex-advertising agency director and his wife, agreed in their evaluation of television news, but on the grounds that they had a shared experience – that of taking a holiday together in Ollerton.

Before drawing any further conclusions on the impact of experience and political culture on belief, we will go first to the remaining residents' groups.

Beckenham residents

Beckenham is adjacent to Bromley and is also a very middle-class area. This group all lived in a well-appointed block of flats. Most were in their late middle age or were now retired. They included people who were working or who had worked as company/shipping secretaries, housewives, or in the civil service; plus a college lecturer, a draper, a personnel officer, and a Salvation Army officer.

On the first visit, thirteen months after the strike, I interviewed eight of these people in a single group. I returned shortly after to see the remaining four. Between them they produced one trade union and three 'BBC' news programmes:

Trade union news

> We are speaking to you from outside Congress House where we hope to interview both Scargill and MacGregor emerging from talks which have broken down yet again, due to the intransigence of the Coal Board.
>
> Today at Bilston Glen colliery there was further confrontation between the police in riot gear and the pickets. Once again the police used strong-armed tactics against lawful, unarmed pickets.
>
> Last night the police displayed pictures of weapons allegedly

taken from peaceful pickets, including a shot-gun, found in the vicinity. Trade union officials vehemently denied the use or possession of such lethal weapons.

MacGregor and Scargill are just emerging.
'Have you any message for us sir?'
'No comment. You will have to refer to my executive for further information.'

First BBC news

Mr MacGregor made another offer to Mr Scargill, which was turned down. The police were brought into the matter and produced a shot-gun. Congress House was trying to find a solution.

In spite of all the bad feeling, the villagers carried on funding and collections in London and throughout the country.

Mr Scargill approached the TUC but it was felt that they did not wish to commit themselves.

Second BBC news

Last night when a convoy of lorries were leaving Bilston Glen colliery with coal supplies for the CEGB power stations, thousands of pickets attempted to impede their progress. When hundreds of police tried to clear a path, stones and missiles were hurled at them. The police used their riot shields and charged. Later at the police station, among weapons captured was a shot-gun.

Third BBC news

For weeks now the pit wheels have remained at a standstill during the miners' strike. Crowds of men have gathered outside the pits, airing their views, picketing and in some instances doing battle with the boys in blue – the police.

Everyone is naturally anxious about his own welfare and interests; the futures of family and friends seem bleak. Efforts have also been made to help one another, including a local brass band making a recording which has been put on sale.

Today there have been further talks between the main protagonists, of the National Coal Board and the NUM – Mr Scargill, regarding the slow return to work which is demonstrated by the figures on the map. This has caused some strife

> in normally happy mining communities, where even relatives have fallen out. (A senior police officer) here shows a shot-gun which was rescued from one man who was threatening to blow out the brains of his younger brother who – because of dire need – had returned to work and broken the strike.

This was again a fairly conservative group. The tone of much of the discussion was set by remarks which were made when the pictures were first seen. One woman commented: 'Oh, that's the awful Scargill'. Another suggested that 'at one time of course Mr MacGregor was knocked over by this rabble'.

Given the views of most of the group, the trade union news above is close to being a parody. Most of the group did actually believe that the gun belonged to the pickets. But their stories do indicate the memories that have been retained of the strike. There is no significance in the 'brass band' reference in the third BBC news as I explained this picture to this group, since it was causing puzzlement. But again we see that the people have the ability to generate memories, which do not relate to the pictures in any direct way at all. For example, there are references to the 'convoy of lorries' at the power stations, the attitude of the TUC, and divisions within families over the strike. The trade union news uses the word 'intransigence' to describe the attitude of the Coal Board. One member of the Scottish women's group had also commented that this word had stuck in her mind. She had remarked that: 'Intransigence, I was sick of hearing that word'.

The gun and picketing

As we might expect from the news stories, most of the group associated the gun with the pickets. Six people thought this and there were other references to 'rent-a-mob pickets', 'a flying picket', and 'pickets (militant)'. Two did not connect the gun with anyone in the dispute and one associated it with the police.

The attitudes expressed towards the BBC also pointed to the conservative nature of this group. Eight people believed that it was 'balanced', 'neutral', or showed 'the reality'. But one said that it was 'left-wing', another that it was 'not pro-Thatcher', one that it was 'inclined to the left marginally', and one said that it gave 'more opportunity for left-of-centre views'. Such opinions on the 'bias' of television depend very much on what the news is expected to be doing. If the expectation is that it will be supporting 'your side', then the featuring of critical views might be seen as an indication of bias. The woman who said that the BBC was 'not pro-Thatcher' also expressed surprise at this, saying that she thought 'it would have been more so'. But it is also possible to understand the job of television news as being to feature a range of views. Audiences can then make judgements about which of these are most prominently featured. Such judgements are not always informed simply by individual political beliefs. As we have seen there are several people in the sample as a whole who believed that the BBC news was 'to the right', while describing themselves in the same way.

On the issue of picketing in the strike, this group featured a remarkable number of people who believed that it was mostly violent. Ten out of the twelve people believed this. Four of them qualified their answer slightly by saying that the strike had started peacefully but they believed that most of what had taken place overall was violent. The source of these beliefs was given as television and the press, with the emphasis being once again upon television news. There were comments made such as 'all TV – I don't take much notice of what I read in the papers'. Another said that she preferred her paper because when she was fed up with it she could throw it away. But she thought television made the biggest impression because 'it kept thumping it at you – as soon as you turned it on, there it was'. One man did say that he was influenced more by the paper than by television but he then added that 'the pictures of horses charging did stick in my mind'.

Two people in the group rejected the television account of picketing. One commented that:

> I try and look behind the news – it may be that violent parts were shown. This perhaps shows a greater proportion of violence than there actually was.

This person had a daughter who lived near to Bilston Glen colliery in Scotland. Each time the strike had come on he had looked to see if the area was featured. He commented that 'we didn't hear much from Bilston Glen, perhaps because there wasn't much violence there'.

The second person in this group to reject the television view was a woman who was in the Salvation Army. She lived with her mother, who was now elderly and who was herself a retired Salvation Army officer. The mother had believed that picketing was mostly violent and had thought that television showed 'the reality'. The daughter expressed some surprise at her mother's view and gave two reasons for her doubts. One related to her experience of living in a mining area:

> As a child I grew up in Durham and knew a lot of people in mining communities and they were very decent people who wouldn't have got involved in violence.

She gave another reason which related to her own understanding of television:

> With a TV camera you can take one shot and make it look like 100 shots. You can take it from one angle and make it look like there are hundreds fighting – in short cheat shots and manipulation.

She had read of this in a religious book, which had used the analogy of the manipulation of film images to comment on personal morality. As she said 'if you didn't live your life correctly, you were doing cheat shots'. The example which the book had used was of stunt photography in Hollywood. But the woman had applied the analysis to television coverage of picketing and had decided that it was a 'cheat shot'. Her conclusion had in part been influenced by her experiences of mining areas. But of course it does not follow that everyone with such experience would form the same conclusion. In this instance, the mother seemed to be more reliant upon the television images. They had no direct experience of the strike and neither did anyone else in this group.

Memories and beliefs

The answers to question 7 show something of the attitudes to the miners' leader. Half of the group thought that 'Arthur Scargill' or 'Arthur Scargill's rabble-rousing' or 'Arthur Scargill on screen' was the topic most shown during the strike. The other half of the group answered 'picketing' or 'violence'.

The answers to question 8 were indicative of more complex divisions within the group:

Question 8 (most personal impact)

1 Hardship to wives and children
2 Scargill
3 Look of hate on men's faces throwing bricks.
4 Use of police horsemen against miners and fear on people's faces when they were used
5 Terrible weapons used, nails driven into wood (pickets) concrete hurled, nuts and bolts under horses' hooves
6 Violence to families of returning miners
7 Horses, miners (violence)/families
8 Violence, smashed heads of police
9 Intimidation and sending your neighbours to Coventry – also the community spirit that went on and the way in which women organized soup kitchens, rallied round their men
10 Terrible intimidation that goes on – absolute fear that was put into those that went to work
11 Men milling around, agitation/going back to work, marching behind bands – took me back to my childhood, to Gala day, which was something really special
12 The women threw whatever they could and shouted at their neighbours

Some of these memories do relate to personal experience. The respondent who is numbered 11 in the list is the Salvation Army member who had spoken of living in Durham. The final return to work had evoked images from her own childhood. Her mother remembered the behaviour of women to their neighbours. As Christian people, both mother and daughter said they thought this was not how people should behave.

These are important examples of how perception can be influenced by belief and personal history. The same pictures which had engendered such happy memories of the miners' gala had reduced a woman from another group (a London Transport catering worker) to tears, because of their connotations in the loss of the strike.

We can also see evidence here of another important filter on perception and memory. The respondent in the list who is numbered 9 highlights the role of the women in the strike. She is shocked by the strong emotions generated within the communities, but at the same time is impressed by the spirit of the people and especially by the way in which the women 'rallied round their men'. She seems to identify with the situation as a woman herself, which is very interesting since she has no time at all for the miners' leader, Arthur Scargill, or what she refers to as his 'rabble-rousing'. In this case the two filters of gender and political belief seem to be producing different impressions of the strike.

In the rest of the replies, we can see some of the strongly negative feelings which existed in the group. There is the sense of shock at the 'hate' and 'violence'. The weapons used by the pickets and the injuries to the police come high in some of the memories. However, the respondent numbered 4 remembered the way in which police horses were used and the fear which this caused. This was an interesting response as this person also referred to a personal experience of the police which had obviously been very distressing to him. He found it very difficult to talk about, but said:

> I was stopped by the police for something I didn't even know I was doing. They spoke to me as if I was a little boy.

In the group as a whole, there were some strong negative opinions voiced about the police. This surprised me, given the composition of the group. Four expressed very positive opinions. Two people said there was no change in their attitudes and one that the police had changed, but that this had been forced upon them. Five were critical, saying that the police were 'more physical to coloureds and others' and that they were 'no longer incorruptible'. The woman who had spoken of 'Scargill's rabble-rousing' commented that 'they are getting some right wrong-uns in the force now'. Her husband added that:

> I am convinced that there are a percentage of people in the police whose behaviour is giving them a bad name – also I think a percentage are anti-black or anti-coloured – but they have a lot to put up with.

Only the man who had the personal experience of the police linked his beliefs in any way to the strike. Others related their criticisms to the treatment of black people or to specific instances such as the assaults on the six youths in a police van in Islington in 1983. The search for the culprits had become a long-running story until the eventual trial of police officers in 1986.

As a whole, this group placed a relatively high degree of trust in television and drew much of their understanding of the strike from it and to a lesser extent from the press. One of the group said of himself and his wife: 'All our impressions come from the media'. These two people were with the first eight who were interviewed. All of these had believed that most picketing was violent. At the end of this meeting I spoke of the descriptions of picketing which had been given to me by the police and the trade unionists. There was real surprise at this and a feeling in the group that they had been greatly misled by the media. They left the room still discussing it in an animated fashion with comments such as 'Well it shows you doesn't it?'

Shenfield residents, Essex

Shenfield is an urban area outside London, but which has grown rapidly because of its road and rail links with the capital. It is something of a middle-class dormitory suburb and many of its residents journey each day to London. It has a Conservative MP and local authority. But the area has become associated with 'soft' toryism and the local authority has been prominent in criticizing some aspects of national government policy.

Writing the news

It was fourteen months after the strike had ended. This group of ten people were mostly aged between 30 and 50, with one 18-year-old and one person in his 60s. Two people requested that they go into the BBC group and one asked if she could write an ITN news. No one volunteered for the trade union group, so the people who produced this were simply allocated to it.

BBC news

As the drift back to work in the mines began to gather momentum, violence erupted, directed against the homes and families of so-called scabs.

(A senior police officer) of the South Yorkshire police expressed concern at the intimidation of strikebreakers and showed evidence of the weapons that were being used to defend themselves and their families. (Gun shown),

A stern-faced Arthur Scargill questioned about such incidents as he left Congress House at the end of a late night meeting, refused to comment.

A confident Mr MacGregor was more forthcoming and condemned the violence but praised the courage of the returning miners. He was, however, concerned at the irreparable damage done to some pits which would never be able to re-open.

Meanwhile, in hard-line areas, miners' wives expressed strong support for their striking husbands and were in the forefront of demonstrations.

ITN news

Twelve miners returned today at Bilston Glen colliery, despite a pit-head meeting addressed by Arthur Scargill, the NUM President. By a show of hands the meeting agreed to remain on strike. The prolonged strike is now entering its 45th week and money to support the strike action is being raised by local events.

The police chief inspector for the area showed weapons which had been found at the scene where picketing had taken place. Police in riot gear were out in large numbers to ensure that the 12 men wishing to work gained passage to the pit.

Mr MacGregor said 'I am always willing to negotiate but I am not prepared to shift the position the management have taken which has the full weight of the law.'

Trade union news

As the miners' strike continues, Mr Scargill emerged from a meeting of NUM leaders in Congress House to say that despite the claims by MacGregor that miners were returning to the pits, support for the struggle was still solid.

Pit-head meetings were fully attended and confirmed the determination to continue the fight. Wives demonstrated their support in many areas. Pop groups and others were busy raising money to sustain the miners.

Despite the vast police presence and many incidents of police brutality against peaceful pickets our members remained solid behind their leaders.

Senior police officers have tried to incriminate pickets by producing false evidence of the use of firearms and other weapons.

MacGregor's claims of miners returning to work are obvious fabrications.

The language of some of these stories relates closely to the actual news as, for example, in the reference to 'the drift back to work'. The stories also featured several themes which were generated independently of the pictures, such as the references to wives demonstrating their support, pit-head meetings, and violence against 'the homes and families' of non-strikers.

The use of individual pictures was interesting. The picture of the woman seated in the crowd (Picture 7, page 16) was used by the BBC group to illustrate miners' wives being 'in the forefront of demonstrations'. The same picture was then discussed by the ITN group as a possible illustration for the 'anger' in the strike. These were what the pictures meant at first to different individuals. As we have seen, sometimes these meanings change as people argued about the 'intrinsic' content of a picture.

But it was also possible for the pictures to be used to illustrate ways of understanding the strike which some in the group did not actually agree with. The above trade union news is in some respects close to that produced by the groups of trade unionists who supported the strike. But it was clear that some of those who produced this trade union news regarded what they had written as a parody. The person who read it out put on a 'funny' Yorkshire/trade union style voice while doing it. As we have already seen, people can understand and reproduce the key elements of points of view which they do not themselves share. It is a short step from this to making judgements about which views are most typically featured in the news. As we have seen, such judgements are not always determined simply by personal commitment.

This group included people with a range of political opinions. But in their judgements on the BBC, no one here assessed it as being 'left-wing'. One person thought that the BBC was 'balanced' and one said that no news was totally unbiased. The rest of the group believed that the BBC was 'establishment', 'government's view', 'right-wing', or 'slightly biased to Conservatives'. These views of the BBC were held by some whose beliefs in other areas would not be regarded as left-wing. For example, one of the group was an accountant, who had a very positive view of the police and who believed that what was mostly shown on

18 Shenfield residents

television news during the strike was 'the rantings and ravings of Arthur Scargill'. But his view of the BBC was that it 'tends towards the establishment, i.e. government, viewpoint'.

The questions – the gun and picketing

On the issue of the gun, most believed that it belonged to striking miners or pickets. Five thought this and one said it was the property of a left-wing activist on a picket line. There were a variety of other answers with one person believing that it belonged to a local farmer and had been planted by someone trying to stir up trouble, another thought it belonged to the police, another to ' "scabs" for self-defence' and one did not associate its ownership with any group in the strike.

The beliefs about picketing showed clearly how people could use indirect experience to criticize news coverage. Six of the group believed that picketing was mostly peaceful, three that it was mostly violent, while one was unsure. Those who thought it was mostly violent cited television and the press as the source of their beliefs. One of the group, a headmaster in a comprehensive school, wrote that his opinion 'derived mainly from what was shown on TV news and what newspapers drew attention to'.

Those who rejected the television account pointed to differences between its coverage of picketing and reports in the quality press/journals such as the *Economist* and reports on local radio. But three of the group also had indirect experience which they drew upon. One had spoken with people who were involved in the dispute and had parents who lived in south Wales. Two of the group had contacts with the police. One, who was a housewife, wrote that she had 'spoken to people with husbands and sons in the police force, working many hours overtime, who say that the picketing was peaceful'. Another in the group was a student who described how her own opinion had changed:

> The picketing reported was how I saw the strike; I saw it as violent to start with, but by meeting a policeman that I knew, I was informed that in his view most was peaceful. None of his mates [in the police] saw any violence.

Memories and beliefs

Personal experience also had some influence on memories of the strike. But we also see here again the extraordinary impact of the media persona of Arthur Scargill:

	Question 7 (on news most)	**Question 8 (most personal impact)**
1	Picketing	Confrontation and the change of use of the police from 'bobbies' to National Guards and 'riot squads'
2	Scargill v. MacGregor arguments	Groups of angry men standing jeering and calling at the 'scabs' or miners returning to work/the number of people who were willing to help others, food parcels
3	Violent scenes	Police charging and beating people

4	The rantings and ravings of Arthur Scargill	The incredibly naive and incompetent leadership of the miners and the poor public relations of MacGregor
5	Arthur Scargill	The despair, anger, and bitterness of the men who lost their jobs/the hopelessness of their families – shortage of money
6	Arthur Scargill, who never listened to anybody else's point of view	Arthur Scargill's power over the hardworking, innocent followers – I found it frightening how he could incite such bitterness – causing families to break up
7	Arthur Scargill rarely seemed to be off the screen	The extent to which the views of the ordinary miners were not given a chance to influence the actions of their leaders – bitterness and violence it engendered are very vivid in my memory
8	Violence/A. Scargill	The dislike Arthur Scargill and Ian MacGregor had for each other – very bitter enmity which pervaded the whole dispute/overall despair/*no* communication
9	Arthur Scargill	Total waste of time as the pits are being shut anyway – the miners didn't win/Arthur Scargill's lost cause/Scargill v. MacGregor/Thatcher/miners lost out
10	(unsure)	Continual exposure of Scargill and MacGregor/the 'play-acting' in front of cameras by pickets

Arthur Scargill is named in eight out of ten of these replies, some of which show an extraordinary depth of hostility. There is none of the 'familiar dislike' which was encountered occasionally in Scotland. Some of the replies here are closer to a sense of moral outrage. But it is interesting that some of the most bitter attacks on Scargill also show strands of sympathy for what is seen as the ordinary miner, described in one reply (number 6) as 'hardworking' and 'innocent'. The fifth reply highlights the despair of those who have lost their jobs and the shortage of money caused by the strike. We have seen elsewhere how such a reply can correlate with class experience. The woman who wrote this was the wife of the accountant who was quoted above. I asked her if she had ever been unemployed or if anyone in her family had been. She replied:

> I am Welsh. When I was three I came to London because my father was out of work in the Depression (in 1931). I suppose it was connecting that in my mind. I have heard about the situation in those days. My uncles and my grandfather worked in the steelworks in south Wales. They tend to be the sort of person who are affected, when you have a recession.

This experience seems to have shaped her perception and memory of events which took place many years later. It did so without her being consciously aware of it – as she said, she was not thinking of her family history when she wrote the reply.

Different forms of experience had affected some of the group's attitude to the police. Overall, six people said that their attitude had become more negative since the strike, two said there was no change, and two said that their attitude was now more positive and that they had added sympathy for the police. One of these was the accountant quoted above, who had close working contacts with the police as he was seconded to the Department of Public Prosecutions. He wrote that working closely with the police had given him practical experience of the difficulties which they faced.

A very different indirect contact was cited by the respondent numbered 6 above to explain her change in attitude. She wrote that a close acquaintance had been stopped by the police on a minor motoring offence and was 'treated in an extremely rude and aggressive way'. This seems to have affected her perception of the use of force by the police, and left her with a very ambivalent attitude. As she wrote:

> In some cases today, they seem to use unnecessary force even though I feel they are very much provoked. On the whole I think they do a difficult job well. The police have become more aggressive.

This attitude is in some ways reminiscent of that of the solicitor in the Glasgow office, who was in the Territorial Army. His comments oscillated in a similar way, based on contradictory elements of experience and belief.

This group also gives us further examples of how the news was understood within single family units. The respondents numbered 1, 2, and 3 are a wife, daughter, and husband respectively. Only the daughter cites the direct experience of knowing the policemen as the source of her understanding of picketing. The respondents numbered 4 and 5 are the accountant and his wife, who brought her own very specific experience to her memory of the events. By contrast, those numbered 6 and 7 are a husband and wife who have very similar memories of the strike and views of picketing as being mostly violent.

Both gave their source of information as television and the press. Those numbered 8 and 9 are a husband and wife who give different views on picketing. The wife cites television coverage for her belief that it is mostly violent, while the husband rejects this, quoting the experience of speaking with people involved and with his parents in South Wales.

The pattern which seems to be emerging here is that where people rely on television and the press for information, there is a relatively uniform interpretation of the news on issues such as the nature of picketing. But the experience and cultural dimensions which people bring to their understanding of news can produce wide variations in belief and memory within the groups and indeed within single families. We can pursue this further in the general conclusions.

6

Conclusions: news content and audience belief

This chapter summarizes the results of the study and shows how the new programmes written by the groups compare with actual news broadcasts.

The news writing exercise: the groups

The range of groups in the study was not large enough to make generalizations about the whole population. But the groups were sufficiently varied to highlight some sharp differences in political culture, class, and personal experience. It was remarkable how quickly some of the groups established the parameters of their own political culture. With the Glasgow women, for example, the presentation of a 'BBC news' was greeted by calls of 'they tell lies, the BBC' and 'ITN was worse'. By contrast, members of the Beckenham residents' group established a very different tone, by making remarks on 'the awful Scargill'. Such comments revealed what was assumed to be 'known' by the group and also what was assumed to be 'acceptable'. It was not simply cultural competence which was being displayed here but also an element of cultural policing. The assumed political culture could exert considerable pressure on anyone who disagreed. This in itself is an important reason for interviewing people individually as well as in groups. The early stages of this study had included a pilot discussion with a group of people from St Albans, Hertfordshire. This is a relatively conservative area in the south-east of the country. One of the women in the group had originally lived in a mining town in Lancashire. In the discussion she said that she thought the gun belonged to an 'outsider with the pickets'. But speaking with me later she said that she had thought the gun might have been a 'police plant'. She had not liked to say so as she assumed that she would be the only one who believed this. She said that she had been brought up 'Labour' and sympathized with them, but 'didn't like to say so in St Albans'.[1]

Differences in political culture and class experience had important influences in the interpretation of news. This could be seen in the way in which the pictures were used in the writing of the news stories. The seated woman in Picture 7 (page 16) was seen by some as being angry but by others as looking anxious and concerned. Similarly the pictures of the crowd scenes could be 'seen' in different ways according to different assumptions about the strike. But the meaning of these pictures was not indefinitely negotiable. There is of course a cultural basis to perception in the sense that what we 'see' and understand is conditioned by pre-existing assumptions. But we do not live in a culturally sealed space in which all the interpretations which we make of images and of new information which we receive are determined by a fixed set of prior beliefs. My argument is that our beliefs may have contradictory elements within them and one source of such contradiction is that our experiences do not always match our expectations. In this study it was apparent that sometimes the pictures didn't fit very well with the beliefs and assumptions which were being brought to them. The perceptual process might begin with someone picking up Picture 8 (page 16) and speaking of it as denoting 'angry mobs' (as in the Glasgow solicitors' office). But that definition has then to be defended when others point out that the people don't look angry and are just standing around. The discussion which ensues relates in part to what is argued to be the empirical content of the picture. Our perception is not insulated against the processes by which people try to win our consent to 'see' the world in a given way. The information which we receive and indeed the pictures which we are shown are crucial dimensions to the formation of our understanding, albeit that our minds are not simply *tabulae rasae* or empty vessels to be filled with a preferred viewpoint.

We have seen that some groups did establish a fairly uniform cultural ethos which included an accepted account of the strike. But in other groups the account was more openly contested and part of the argument involved how the empirical content of the pictures was to be understood. This raises important questions for theoretical positions which suggest that what is 'seen' is determined simply by prior belief.

Group news and television news

The pictures had the effect of stimulating a flow of memories and 'news language', which was often very close to that of the actual news. The stories could not be generated in this way unless there was already a very clear appreciation of the central themes in news reporting. Some of the themes which were included such as the role of miners' wives, arguments within families, and the economics of pit closures had no direct referents in the pictures at all. But even the pictures which may seem most evocative of the events in the strike only appear as such to us because of the cultural knowledge which we have already imbued. This was tested with a group of American students who had not been in Britain at the time of the strike. They attempted the news-writing exercise using the same pictures. Only one of twenty-eight people could identify a picture of Arthur Scargill and in general they had very little prior knowledge of the issues involved. In the news accounts which they produced, one group effectively gave up and wrote a story on the '*minors*' strike', using the pictures for a spoof story about children who refused to grow up. Nine of the group had some memories of having seen references to the strike on American television. All that they could remember were scenes of violence, and they said that this would have been the content of the story or it would not be shown in the US. Some of these produced a more credible news account of a strike:

> Kiverton Park was also the scene of further violence, as another strike demonstration erupted into street rioting.
>
> Police were called upon to restore order at the strike site, but were drawn into the riot. Three police were injured as the strikers stormed the gates of the Congress House.
>
> The Congress House was the meeting place for trade union leaders and mining companies to negotiate wage increases and future benefits for the striking miners.
>
> The miners were unhappy with the mining companies; which was their justification given for the street riot.
>
> Looting around the area was prominent as police were engaged with trying to contain the riot itself.
>
> (US students, 26.3.86)

What they have done is to situate an American labour dispute into a British context. The NCB disappears and is replaced by the private 'mining companies' negotiating 'wage increases'. Picket-line violence goes, to be replaced by 'street riots' and 'looting', as the gates of Congress House are stormed.

Compare this with one produced by a group of first-year students at Glasgow University. This was written in November, 1987, over two and a half years after the strike had ended.

BBC news

Ten months into the miners' strike, picket-line violence reached new heights when police found a number of weapons at (a colliery) in North Yorkshire.

Clashes began early in the day and continued into the afternoon resulting in police reinforcements being brought in from south Yorkshire. During a series of bitter attacks from both sides, police retrieved a number of weapons, amongst which was a double-barrelled shot-gun.

The Yorkshire chief of police commented on the incident saying the finding of firearms was an alarming development.

(Police officer): 'Quite frankly this is a frightening turn of events. The brave British bobbies, many of whom have young families, are facing in the line of duty armed extremists with no sense of law and order. The public can rest assured that we will not rest on this matter until it has been fully investigated and the culprits have been brought to justice.'

Miners' leader Arthur Scargill commented from meetings in Congress House on the situation, saying that while he condemned this discovery, he could not accept that responsibility lay wholly on the miners on the picket line. He stressed that these disturbances were typical examples of police trying to incite violence on the picket lines. He also said that he found it impossible to believe that his members would resort to this kind of violence – and he could only suggest that it was the work of outside elements brought in by the NCB to force strikers back to work. He concluded that this isolated incident was totally blown out of proportion by the media.

NCB chairman, Ian MacGregor, was quick to comment on the

> incident, angrily rejecting Mr Scargill, saying that his claim was despicable in view of such a frightening discovery. He also said that this incident was typical of the disruptions that we have seen throughout the strike, employed to reverse the flow of strikers back to work. And he was sure that the police in their role of peacemakers will continue to do their utmost to protect the innocent workers from these kinds of 'bully-boy' tactics.

Many of these themes have a familiar ring from earlier groups, such as 'picket-line violence', 'the flow of striking miners back to work' and the arguments between Scargill and MacGregor. Some news themes and specific language from the strike have passed very deeply into cultural memories. The ability of people to reproduce accounts which are so close to the actual news is quite remarkable. Consider, for example, the statement attributed to Ian MacGregor in the above story where he speaks of 'the disruptions . . . employed to reverse the flow of strikers back to work' and the police doing 'their utmost to protect the innocent workers from these kinds of "bully-boy" tactics'.

Compare this with an actual statement made by Ian MacGregor during a televised debate with Arthur Scargill, shown on Channel 4 news. In this, he commented that:

> I have every indication that the bulk of [miners] want to go back to work – the only reason they are not there is because his bully-boys continue to intimidate them and their families.
> (Channel 4 news, 22.8.88)

If we look at the 'quote' from Arthur Scargill in the above story he is reported by the students as saying 'these disturbances were typical examples of police trying to incite violence on the picket lines' and that 'he found it impossible to believe that his members would resort to this kind of violence'. Compare this with an actual statement made by him in a BBC interview, when defending miners against allegations of pit gear being deliberately damaged:

> I'm concerned that there are well organized and disciplined gangs of police drafted in from all over Britain to try and prevent miners talking to miners . . . I have no evidence and I don't think you have any evidence . . . I repeat that the people responsible for the problems we are now facing, not only in

> South Yorkshire but in Nottinghamshire, are the thousands of police, a national riot police force which have now been drafted in to this part of the world.
>
> (BBC1, 21.00, 22.8.84)

The arguments between Scargill and MacGregor and the long-protracted negotiations were featured in the stories of several of the groups. For example, 'discussions broke down between Scargill and MacGregor' (electronics workers), 'meetings with MacGregor were held at TUC headquarters, talks broke down' (London Transport supervisors), 'meanwhile, against a background of no movement between the parties to break the deadlock . . .' (Glasgow solicitors), and 'another meeting . . . finished abruptly with more arguments and no decisions reached' (Penge women). Some key memories of the strike had also been of 'endless futile discussions' and the word 'intransigence' (Glasgow woman) and of '*no* communication' (Shenfield resident). Compare these examples with the tone of this BBC news report which summarized some of the events in the dispute:

> Agreement remained as far away as ever – the TUC insisted on talks, once again they went badly. The TUC tried to negotiate a better deal but the miners rejected the new proposals from the Coal Board.
>
> (BBC1, 21.10, 3.3.85)

One of the arguments between the miners' union and the Coal Board had been over the 'return to work' and the number of miners who had given up the strike. One of the groups wrote for example that 'today the NCB announced figures on the operational pits . . . Arthur Scargill, the President of the Union, at a meeting in Congress House disputed the figures put out by the NCB' (electronics workers). On the actual news we heard that:

> The Coal Board says a record number of miners ended their strike today. Arthur Scargill says the figures are being mixed like cocktails.
>
> (headline, BBC1, 18.00, 4.2.85)

These arguments were a recurring theme on the news. Three months earlier ITN had reported that:

> 350 more miners returned to work today, last Tuesday 936 went back – the miners' union disagrees with the figures.
> (ITN, 17.45, 27.11.84)

There are direct parallels here between the language of the group news and that of television. In the Glasgow solicitors' office, for example, a phrase was used on 'miners returning to work at increasing rates every day', while on the actual news, we could hear:

> With the return to work of the drivers and the ever-increasing number of miners going back . . .
> (ITN, 22.00, 12.11.84)

It is remarkable how closely some of the group stories reflect not only the thematic content of the news but also the form of actual programmes. For example, consider this headline from the Scottish trade unionists group: 'On a day that saw an increased drift back to work . . . further violence was taking place at Orgreave power plant'. Now compare it with an actual ITN headline:

> Worst picket violence yet but miners continue their drift back.
> (ITN, 17.45, 12.11.84)

On the BBC we could hear that:

> Today's picketing is clearly intended to show that drift. According to the Coal Board's figures, today has seen by far the largest return to work since the strike began.
> (BBC1, 21.00, 12.11.84)

The link between the 'drift back' and violence was also used by a group from Shenfield:

> As the drift back to work in the mines began to gather momentum, violence erupted, directed against the homes and families of so-called scabs.

The television news offered a recurring commentary on the increasing number of people breaking the strike and the apparently ever increasing level of 'new violence'. This news theme highlights what the current 'record' is for both. As in this BBC bulletin:

> Good evening, the headlines at 6 o'clock. A record number of

> miners have gone back to work. The Coal Board has called the response stupendous and there has been the worst violence so far in the coal fields. . . . *The battle between the miners and the Coal Board created two new records today*. More miners returned to work than on any day since the strike began and their return brought with it the worst violence seen on the picket lines in the thirty-six-week history of the strike. (my italics)

The theme of escalating violence is then taken up by the news reporter on the spot:

> *BBC Reporter*: A dozen Yorkshire pits were the targets for the worst concentrated violence of this dispute so far. . . . It was hit-and-run mob destruction. . . . Outside Hickleton colliery a crowd overturned two cars and set them on fire. They belonged to Coal Board officials at the pit and *their destruction marked another escalation in the bitter struggle* inside Britain's mining industry. (my italics)
>
> (BBC1, 18.00, 12.11.84)

19 'There's been a new development described by the police and Coal Board as "sinister" and "dangerous".' (BBC1, 21.00, 22.8.84)

The stories written by the groups also highlighted the theme of violence and its increasing scale. The details disappear, of where the events have happened or what has been destroyed, but the theme is retained. Compare the above BBC news with these phrases from the groups in the Glasgow solicitors' office:

> Trouble broke out between police and miners today. . . . Increasing violent clashes between pickets and police. . . . There were ugly scenes . . . and what was said to be an alarming escalation of violence. . . . After the trouble had died down a shot-gun was produced by police which they claimed had been taken from the mob.

Both accounts use the word 'mob' and the reference to 'another escalation' in the news programme compares directly with the 'alarming escalation' in the group stories. This theme runs through several groups, who wrote 'violence is escalating' (Bromley women), 'escalating the violence' (Retirement group, Glasgow), and 'as the picketing escalated' (London Transport supervisors). It was argued at the time of the dispute that the emphasis on violence in the news led to a neglect of the miners' case.

At the end of the strike, the BBC news included extensive references to 'battles' and 'confrontation' in its summary of the events:

> . . . the battles around [Orgreave] were some of the worst in British industrial history. They sharply raised the level of violence expected in an industrial dispute. The police response, horses, dogs, and riot shields led to bitter criticism – while in some mining communities relations between police and striking miners approached breakdown.
>
> Violent confrontation between police and pickets was to become an almost nightly occurrence in the most militant Yorkshire mining areas.
>
> Mr Scargill himself was arrested one day and he was taken to hospital on another, struck by a police riot shield he said, tumbled down a bank said the police.
>
> (BBC1, 21.10, 3.3.85)

This account was then challenged by Roy Hattersley, the Deputy Leader of the Labour party, who was in the studio:

> Can I say one thing about the film. It was an enormously prejudicial film. Half of the time was taken up by an account

20 ‘Violent confrontation between police and pickets was to become . . .

21 . . . an almost nightly occurrence . . .

22 . . . in the most militant Yorkshire mining areas.' (BBC1, 21.10, 3.3.85)

> of, and pictures of, violence in the dispute – violence which I deplored and condemned at the time – but there was a case that the miners were fighting for, a case for keeping coal, a case for keeping pits open, a case for keeping jobs, a case for protecting their communities. Not a single word of that appears in the film and I do believe that is a disgraceful way to begin your programme this evening.
>
> (BBC1, 21.10, 3.3.85)

Some of the stories written by the groups dealt with the issues behind the dispute. But as we have seen they focused very largely on the Coal Board's view. For example, the Glasgow women wrote of the effort to 'streamline' the industry:

> A government effort to streamline and make the coal industry economically productive

One of the groups of London Transport supervisors had spoken of 're-shaping':

> Today Coal Board management and union met at Congress House over pit closures and the re-shaping of the industry.

The second group of supervisors attributed this statement to Ian MacGregor:

> MacGregor says closures to come to uneconomic pits.

There were echoes of this in a story by the Bromley residents which included the phrase: 'Mr MacGregor and his threat to close uneconomic pits'. The retirement group in Glasgow had also spoken of many pits being 'uneconomical to run' and 'millions of pounds of tax-payers' money being wasted'.

But in fact the miners' union did not accept the Coal Board's economic analysis and argued that Britain already produced deep-mined coal very efficiently. The apparent cheapness of foreign coal, they argued, came from artificial subsidies. It was also suggested at the time of the strike that the key issue behind government policy was the political and economic pressures for nuclear power. If this energy source was to expand, then coal had to contract.[2] None of this is mentioned in any of the groups' news stories.

This absence of the miners' case relates to more than simply the media's preoccupation with violence. There were additional factors which might explain the dominance of the Coal Board's view, such as the extensive advertising and public relations campaign which it was able to mount, and the reliance of the media on the government and Coal Board as sources of information.[3] But the allegations of violence in the strike were important since, as we have seen, they became part of the Coal Board's case against the mineworkers. As the BBC journalist, Nicholas Jones, writes:

> the NCB thought that public opinion was largely on their side – because of the prominence that the news reports had given to picket line violence, which in turn had helped create a favourable climate for the NCB's policy of keeping the pits open for work.
>
> (Jones, 1986, p. 103)

In this sense it is an important finding that the groups associate violence so strongly with the dispute and that none of them is critical of the Coal Board's view of the economics of the industry, or raise other issues such as nuclear power. Some groups did try to present what was seen as the miners' case. But this came down largely to blaming the police for the violence. This was sometimes written in a parodied form – as with the Beckenham residents who referred to the police using 'strong-armed tactics against lawful, unarmed pickets'. In the more sympathetic groups there are references to the miners fighting 'for their jobs and their future' (Glasgow women). One of the Glasgow retirement groups represent the miners' case as being that 'all pits should remain open'. But this was not, in fact, what they were arguing for.

In theory, the miners would accept the closure of pits only on the grounds of exhaustion or that they were unsafe. But in practice pit closures had been going ahead and capacity was being reduced without strike action.[4] In the twelve months before the strike, twenty pits had been shut. But it was the rate of closure and cuts in output sought by the Board which were the key issues; and crucially how these were seen as signifying the future of the industry. But the groups did not feature any such arguments. Instead, economic logic and rationality is seen as being a prerogative of the Coal Board. This was sustained in a situation where the financial costs of the dispute to the state and to the tax-payer were far greater than the initial economies that the Coal Board had hoped to make.[5]

Finally, we come to the issue of the gun and its use in stories. The actual ITN news item in which it featured was very brief, but this story from the retirement group in Glasgow comes close to it:

> Working miners were obliged to keep weapons to safeguard their families and property

The ITN report went as follows:

> One rebel miner has threatened to take the law into his own hands. [He] has vowed to open fire on pickets who attack his home.
>
> *Working Miner*: I just don't want my windows breaking. All I'm doing is protecting my wife, my property, and myself.
>
> *Journalist*: If it comes to it though would you really use the gun?
>
> *Working Miner*: Yes.
>
> (ITN, 13.00, 22.8.84)

However, the similarity between the news and the group account in this case is comparatively exceptional, since the gun was more frequently associated by the groups with striking miners or pickets. There is a possible contradiction here, since, as we have seen, the group stories commonly replicated the news in areas such as the reporting of violence and the return to work. One obvious point to make is that the actual gun story on ITN was very briefly reported and therefore might be expected to have had a very limited impact on the audience. A more crucial issue is why the gun was so frequently placed with the strikers in the group stories, e.g. 'Shot-gun found on picket line', (Croydon solicitors), 'Violence started on picket lines, weapons started to appear' (London Transport supervisors). The answer seems to be that the gun is seen as a violent symbol, the striking miners are associated with violence and, therefore, the gun is given to them. There can be exceptions to this, as when some audience members regarded the striking miners as so violent that the gun was seen as a legitimate means of defence against them (i.e. to protect homes and families). There were other cases where some people rejected the connection between the striking miners and the gun (for example, through sympathy with the strikers or perhaps because they had not been exposed to British news coverage). But in the group stories as a whole the gun was frequently linked to miners/pickets or to the picket lines. We can now look further at the processes by which these associations were made.

The questions: the gun and the picketing

There is no necessary reason why the gun should be associated with any 'side' in the dispute. No shot-guns were ever reported to have been found on the picket lines and none were fired in anger. The associations that the groups made with the weapon vary and to some extent illustrate the differences in cultural assumptions and experience which existed between them. While most of the black women in the London Transport group associated the gun with the police, most of the Beckenham residents associated it with striking miners or pickets.

Such beliefs would also be likely to vary across national cultures. The American students said that they did not associate the weapon with the police, because they thought of police in terms of 'hand-guns'. They described this as a very 'American answer'. While this study was in progress, a journalist from the Soviet Union visited the research unit in Glasgow. His view of the provenance of the gun was that 'without doubt it would have been with a provocateur', by which he meant an agent of the government who was intending to blacken the cause of the miners. The exercise and the results were also examined in detail by a Nigerian postgraduate student in Glasgow, who had not been in Britain at the time of the strike. Her reaction to the gun was to associate it with the police and it surprised her greatly that people in Britain would link guns with strikers. This is perhaps not an unreasonable response given the low profile that firearms have in British industrial disputes and their virtual absence in this one.

In this study, 10 per cent of the people reflected this view and did not associate the gun with anyone in the strike (see Appendix 2). But many more linked the gun to striking miners and pickets. This is very noticeable if we look at the 'general population' groups, (i.e. excluding the four groups with special knowledge and experience from Chapter 2). In this more general sample, 56 per cent of the people linked the gun in this way.[6] Some people gave improvised explanations on its ownership such as 'rent-a-mob pickets', 'a picket out of bravado' (Beckenham residents), or 'a striking miner shot someone' (print worker).

Differences in political culture and experience produced some clear variations between groups. Amongst the miners, Scottish trade unionists, and print workers, only 16 per cent associated the gun with striking miners or pickets. But 46 per cent of these believed that the gun belonged to the police, either as a weapon or as 'planted' evidence. In the more general population groups only 15 per cent of the people believed this.

It was clear that sympathy with the miners could lead to a rejection of any link between them and the gun. Indeed one of the Scottish trade union groups split over exactly this issue. But it was also the case that this link *was* sometimes made by people who were overtly sympathetic to the miners. It was made, in a sense, in spite of their beliefs. One of the trainee solicitors in Glasgow commented that she had made the connection because of what she had seen on the news. Television, of course, had not actually portrayed the strikers as having guns, but it had linked them very firmly to violence.

Violence and the strike

Some events in the dispute *were* clearly violent. People actually lost their lives. Pickets were run over and crushed and the Welsh taxi-driver died when the concrete block was pushed on to the motorway. In their book on the strike, Martin Adeney of the BBC and John Lloyd of the *Financial Times* comment on the serious clashes between police and pickets at Orgreave and the violence in the Yorkshire villages in the second half of the strike. But they also comment on the probable truth of the assertion that '95 per cent of the time picketing was peaceful'. They talk of the 'ritual push and shove, often enjoyed by the young men on both the police and NUM sides'. They describe an encounter in Yorkshire late in 1984:

> The police line is shoved back, quickly reinforced and heaved back into place. It takes about two minutes, police and pickets disentangle as if emerging from a rugby scrum.
>
> (1986, p. 124)

The press and television are sometimes accused of selectivity in their reporting. The sheer scale of the events in the strike meant that there were very many different stories and incidents which could potentially be highlighted. It is important to grasp the magnitude of the events in order to see how such a process of selection can work. At this time there were 190,000 mine-workers in total. There were also tens of thousands of police and workers from other unions and support groups who were involved in actions at different times in the strike. At Orgreave on 18 June 1984, there were 10,000 pickets present plus a very heavy police presence. Other picketing actions were much smaller, but spread over a very large number of locations. There were 174 pits, plus other sites such as power stations, ports, and steelworks. In such a huge sample of people over such a long period, we might expect to find many varieties of human behaviour. There would be miners trained in first aid, who would pause to help policemen who had fallen (which did happen), and we would find people who would throw bolts and bricks.

The political and economic events which surrounded the strike resulted in a conflict on a scale which had been unknown for many years. The police had a pivotal role in this and were seen as directly antagonistic to the strike by those who were pursuing it. When tens of thousands of police, miners, and their supporters confronted each other in such a stressed period, there was a very real possibility that there would be violent incidents. But it is the relentless focus on these by television and the press, accompanied by the comments on 'escalation' and 'new records', which establishes for many of the audience the belief that violence was a persistent feature of most picketing.

There was a remarkable unanimity of belief amongst the groups in this sample about what had actually been shown. In the general sample, 98 per cent believed that most picketing which they had seen on television news was violent. The remaining 2 per cent either were unsure or believed the picketing shown was 'intimidatory' rather than physically violent. But perhaps what is most remarkable is the number of people who believed that these television images represented the everyday reality of picketing. There was occasionally a fear expressed of even going near a picket line, because of the high levels of physical fighting which were believed to be going on. In all, 54 per cent of the general sample believed that picketing was mostly violent.

The source for these beliefs was overwhelmingly given as television and the press, with the emphasis on TV, because of its immediate and more dramatic quality. Some people also indicated how their attitudes had altered as a result of what they had seen. For example, one of the secretaries in the solicitors' office in Croydon wrote that her opinion of the police had improved because 'you do not realise what they have to put up with'. It was clear that some key elements of belief were being provided by the media. But it would be wrong to see people as being totally dependent on such messages, as if they are simply empty vessels which are being filled up by News at Ten. To accept and believe what is seen on television is as much a cultural act as the rejection of it. Both acceptance and rejection are conditioned by our beliefs, history, and experience. A high degree of trust in the BBC, for example, might result from a knowledge of its history and its peculiar role in British society as an authoritative 'national' voice.

Television news itself works very hard at strategies to win our trust. It scorns the crude editorializing of newspapers and uses presentational techniques which suggest neutrality and balance. Whether the audience actually accepts television's presentation of itself depends very much on what beliefs, experience, and information they bring to what they are shown.

In this sample, some people clearly accepted the television account. But others adapted parts of the message and changed key elements of its meaning. For example, some believed that the strike was mostly violent because of what they had seen on television, but blamed the police for provoking the trouble. They could be quite aware that television news had not explained the origins of the violence in this way. The disjunction between what they had seen and what they believed was explained by saying that television 'only showed violence from miners, not police' (Glasgow woman). In such an example, what is finally believed results from news images being interpreted through beliefs about both the police and television.[7]

In the Glasgow retirement group, we encountered a different negotiation of the television message. In this group, there was a very high degree of trust in television news and most accepted its account of the violent nature of picketing. But there was also a high degree of sympathy with the miners and this contradiction was partly resolved by a focus on 'outsiders, infiltrators, and militants' as the cause of the trouble. This negotiation was not completely successful in rehabilitating the miners, as there was also deep unhappiness expressed about the violence and how it had reflected on the miners' cause.

The process by which people understand a television message depends in part on the beliefs which they bring to it and crucially on how these beliefs are utilized. There were cases amongst the group of electronics staff and the Bromley women where people had a critique of television latent in their beliefs. They stated at first that they thought picketing was mostly violent and then moved away from this position as they began to comment on the nature of television as a medium, with its tendency to select and to focus on the sensational. In these cases, the exercise itself seems to have provided the stimulus for the emergence of this view. But it is important that the belief about picketing had in a sense rested with them, until they were pressed to explain it. These again seem to be examples of the message being absorbed in spite of other beliefs which were held.

Where no critical view of television exists, the likelihood of accepting its account may be very great. One person in the Glasgow retirement group commented that television was the most important source of information and took her opinion of picketing from it because as she said:

Seeing is believing.

We also saw one case in this sample where the acceptance of the television message was underlined by indirect experience. One of the London Transport supervisors had stayed for a period in Yorkshire and had thought that the people there had a very 'them-and-us' attitude. This had led him to accept the television portrayal of picketing. But it was clear that in this study the overwhelming effect of indirect and direct experience was to produce a rejection of the television news account. This was most obvious in the case of people who had been at picket lines, whether police, pickets, or other observers. One interesting case was of the Scottish solicitor who had driven past a picket line during the strike and had compared what he had seen with television coverage of picketing. In the same office, a secretary commented that her experience of seeing how a dispute at Chrysler was treated in the news, had led her to question the coverage of the miners' strike.

In the general sample, 43 per cent believed that picketing was mostly peaceful. When giving reasons, about a third of these based their belief on the experience of knowing or having met policemen or miners. The effect of such experience could traverse class and political culture. We saw for example the two Bromley residents whose views were generally on the right and whose key memory of the strike was of 'Arthur Scargill talking rubbish/lies'. Yet they believed that picketing was mostly peaceful because of their contact with miners and their families whilst on holiday at Ollerton.

A second major reason for doubting television news was the comparison of it with other sources of information, such as the 'quality' and local press or 'alternative' current affairs programmes and radio. About 16 per cent of the general sample made such comparisons. These comments were sometimes linked to remarks on the tendency of television to exaggerate and focus on violence to the exclusion of other events. In the general sample, 14 per cent of the people made this criticism and gave it as a reason for rejecting the news presentation. This is a relatively low proportion given that it is sometimes thought that beliefs about the tendency of media to exaggerate are generally held in the population. It might in fact be that they are. But what is significant about this result is that even where such beliefs existed they were not always used to discount what was seen in the news. It was also noteworthy that where people relied only on this criticism to reject the news account, there was a tendency to estimate the level of violence as being very high. Some of the group in the Glasgow solicitors' office made such estimates, although their conclusion was that for a majority of the time picketing was probably peaceful.

These criticisms of television as a medium and the comparison of it with other accounts were made by people with varied political views. But there was another strand of criticism which saw the focus on violence as a conscious attempt to denigrate the miners' case.

This view was most prominent amongst the Scottish trade unionists. One of the London Transport supervisors had also commented that the media 'picked out the violence so as to get the majority of people against the miners'. The trade unionists had criticized several aspects of news presentation, such as the 'big thing' that was made of Ian MacGregor being knocked over and the focus on 'violence instead of support groups'. There was a strong belief amongst them that picketing was mostly peaceful. In arguing this, some also commented on the scale of the strike and the numbers involved, saying that people could not have been fighting most of the time. This deduction could apparently be made irrespective of sympathies with the strike. One woman in the Penge group said that she would have shot striking miners (has she been a working miner), but also argued that, 'because of the amount who were actually on strike . . . it can't all have been violent'. One of the print workers commented that 'if they had been really violent, the police couldn't have coped, it would have been the army' and a Bromley resident said that 'there would be a revolution'.

In the general sample, about 6 per cent of the people gave such deductions as an explanation for their beliefs on picketing, while 3 per cent gave their personal conviction that most people are not inclined to violence. These are relatively small proportions of the sample. We might remember that 54 per cent had believed that most picketing was violent. The source of this belief seems very clearly to have been the media. It is something of an indictment of news journalism that after coverage virtually every day for a year, such a large proportion of people had apparently no idea what a typical picket line was like. The eye-witness accounts which we have seen here were greeted with genuine surprise by many in the groups who had been convinced by what they had seen on the news.

Memory and beliefs

The most frequently cited memories were of violence. Seventy-two per cent of the general sample thought that 'confrontation', 'clashes', 'picketing', and 'violence' were what was shown most on television news of the strike (see Appendix 2). In the key memories, 'confrontation', 'violence', and 'picketing' were again cited more than any other issue. These were given by 27 per cent of the people in the general sample. There were other issues cited as key memories which had connotations of violence, such as the intimidation/treatment of non-strikers (6 per cent), police violence/causing trouble/charging miners on horseback (12 per cent), and the death of the Welsh taxi-driver (9 per cent). Arthur Scargill was named as being what was 'most shown' by 27 per cent of the general sample and was given as a key memory by 21 per cent, sometimes accompanied by pejorative comments. This was most noticeable in the south of the country. In the Shenfield group, for example, the miners' leader is named in eight out of the ten replies. For some respondents he was thought to be both what was shown most on television and also had the greatest impact upon them of anything in the strike. This suggests that judgements about the content of news were being affected by prior belief, in this case the intense antipathy which was felt for Scargill.

The assessment of what was on the news most could also be affected by direct involvement or close sympathy with the dispute. The Scottish trade unionists, the Yorkshire miners, and the printers in Fleet Street all included references to the return to work.

They had generally a very cynical view of the media and many saw the news emphasis on the breakdown of the strike as evidence of bias against the miners' cause. As one miner put it, television had shown 'returning miners, the more the better'. But the images were clearly also very significant in their own memories, because of what they represented in terms of the failure of union solidarity. This was very apparent in the case of the print workers who were involved in their own union dispute. For some in these groups, the return to work was given as the key memory of the strike and was also estimated to have been the issue most shown on the news. But there was not always such a clear correspondence between these two dimensions of memory. Some respondents made clear distinction between them. In the general sample, 9 per cent believed that negotiations, meetings, and arguments featured most in news coverage, but there were no references to these as key memories.

As we have seen, for most people the violent images were very salient and were thought to have predominated in the news. But many also made it clear that there were other memories which had an even more powerful impact upon them. For example the group of Scottish trade unionists had believed overwhelmingly that violence was the most shown issue on the news. But nearly half of the group did not include this in their key memories and instead spoke of the role of support groups and miners' wives and the attitude of the government and the Coal Board.

In the general sample, memories were clearly affected by political belief and class experience. The groups of women in Glasgow and Penge remembered people queueing for food and the loss of jobs in the dispute. But class experience was not synonymous with political belief. Some of the middle-class women in Bromley were very sympathetic to the miners' cause – yet none of these gave unemployment or hardship in the strike as a key memory.

The effect of experience on perception could apparently last for many years. One of the middle-class residents of Shenfield gave as her key memory of the strike the hopelessness of families and 'shortage of money'. She explained this by speaking of the harsh consequences of unemployment on her family when she was a small child.

Attitudes to police action in the strike could also be affected by past experience. One woman in the Glasgow retirement group commented on her belief that the police were 'causing the trouble' during the strike. She based this view on experiences when living in a large working-class housing estate, twenty years earlier. There were several examples of how direct contact with the police could have remarkable effects on memories of the dispute. Two people from the middle-class areas of Bromley and Beckenham gave 'police tactics' and 'use of police horsemen against miners and fear on people's faces', as their key memories of the strike. Both also gave accounts of how they had been stopped by the police – one of them for what was described as an 'April Fool's joke'.

In the general sample as a whole, there was apparently a growth in negative attitudes towards the police. Forty-three per cent of the people said that their attitude had changed for the worse in the period since the strike, while 11 per cent said that their attitude had improved (a further 12 per cent said that their attitude was already very good). Some of these changes in attitude related to media coverage of events which had nothing to do with the miners' dispute – such as the attack on the six youths in a police van in Islington in 1983 and the subsequent action against police officers.

Criticisms of the police which were featured in the media could sometimes be re-negotiated by people who were sympathetic with the force. They might say for example that the tougher stance of the police was being 'forced upon them', or the criticisms might simply be rejected. But negative contact with the police seemed to have a very powerful impact on the beliefs of people who might otherwise have been sympathetic.

This further underlines one of the key findings here, that direct experience can have a crucial influence of how new information from the media is understood. Such direct contacts, together with political culture, class experience, processes of logic, and comparisons made between accounts, were the most important factors in the relation between perception and belief.

These findings show that some of the media audience clearly negotiate the meaning of what they are told. However, the influence of media and especially television was central, since it established so firmly the issues which came to be associated with the strike. Some of these, such as the emphasis on violence and the return to work, were very damaging to the miners' cause. Those who sought to reject these accounts of the strike had in a sense to struggle against the dominant flow of images from the media. For those without access to direct experience, it was sometimes a losing battle.

There is some sense of this constant flow of relatively uniform images in the account by Gerbner *et al.* (1986) of television's contribution to conceptions of social reality. The term 'cultivation' is used to describe media influence as a gravitational process:

> . . . cultivation is not conceived as a unidirectional process but rather more like a gravitational process. The angle and direction of the 'pull' depends on where groups or viewers and their styles of life are in reference to the center of gravity, the 'main stream' of the world of television. Each group may strain in a different direction, but all groups are affected by the same central current. Cultivation is thus part of a continual, dynamic, on-going process of interaction among messages and contexts.
> (1986, p. 24)

It has been argued that there are methodological problems with the work of Gerbner *et al.* in that they do not adequately analyse the specific meanings which are being conveyed by television messages. For example, the Gerbner group assume that the content of fictional television offers a relatively uniform message. They measured the effect of such programmes on audience beliefs by comparing the views of those who watched comparatively little television with those who were heavy consumers of it (Gerbner *et al.*, 1978, 1979, and 1986). Wober and Gunter (1988) have argued that such an approach does not allow for potential differences between areas of television content or for the possibility of contradictory messages, between or within programmes. The value of the method which I have tried to develop in this volume is that it does show specifically the meanings which audiences associate with television news and the sources of the different elements which contribute to audience beliefs. Television is not the only influence, but this book does point to its very crucial role.

The next chapter shows how these conclusions relate to other areas of media studies – specifically, to the analysis of media content, to the debate on media effects, and to the current controversy over 'media bias'.

7

Issues in news content, effects, and 'bias'

News content

The approach of asking people to write their own news programmes revealed very clearly the themes which had been retained in their memories. These themes and the language in which they were expressed were stimulated by the sight of the pictures which were used. But the pictures could not of themselves produce this news language. In practice, they triggered the responses and revealed systems of belief which were already in existence. Their relative ambiguity meant that they could be used to illustrate different themes. For example, the map with numbers on it was used both to discuss the return to work and to indicate how many pits were operational.

The important issue here is the clarity with which such themes were recalled and the close correspondence between descriptions in the group news and actual news programmes. We have seen for example how some groups were able to reproduce not only the thematic content of news bulletins on issues such as violence, but also the structure and language of actual news headlines.

This study is not primarily intended as a content analysis of television news. But it will be useful to illustrate how some key themes were developed and highlighted in television coverage. Several theorists have already written on the treatment of violence as an issue in the news. L. Masterman analysed news coverage of the conflict between pickets and police at Orgreave in June 1984 (Masterman, 1986, p. 106). He showed how violence was initially blamed on the miners in BBC news coverage and how this explanation began to change as other programmes revealed details of police actions.[1]

Television news and the 'drift back'

The return to work was another key issue in arguments over media coverage. We have seen how the miners and other trade unionists saw the treatment of this as crucial. For them the images of the return symbolized the breaking of the strike and were a central feature of what they saw as a biased media presentation. Some journalists also commented on how the Coal Board's view of the return and phrases such as 'the drift back' became a routine part of news coverage. Michael Crick from ITN's Channel 4 news published his own diary of the strike:

> November. The National Coal Board's skilful propaganda claims that men are returning daily in hundreds, even thousands, and detailed figures are supplied first thing to news desks every day. Some journalists don't bother to attribute the figures to the Board . . . and most have generally adopted the Board's phrase 'the drift back' despite its suggestions of a continuous and inevitable process.
>
> (Crick, 1985)

Illustration 23 shows the use of the 'drift back' theme in ITN's news coverage in November 1984. But the theme in fact recurs

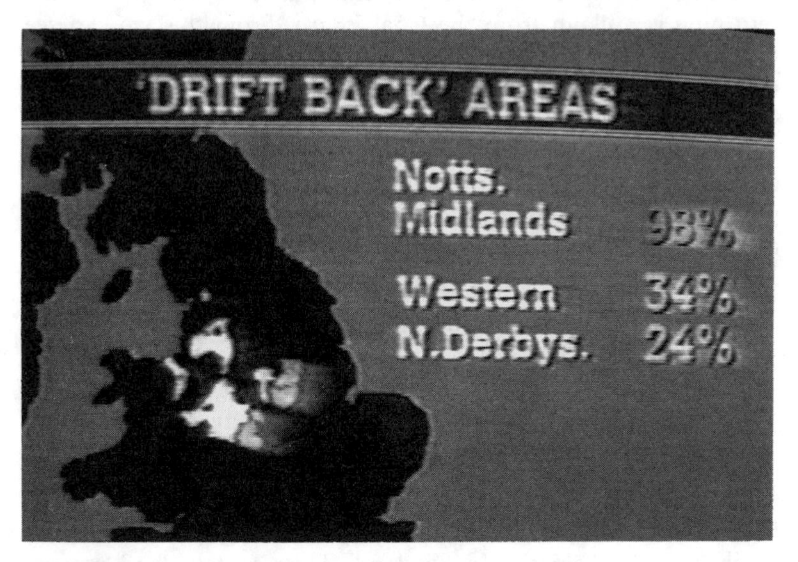

23 ITN, 22.00, 12.11.84

in the news over long periods during the strike and became a central element in the organization of coverage.[2] If we look in detail at a bulletin from this period we can see how the return to work is highlighted.

On 7 January 1985 the BBC began its evening news with these headlines:

> Good evening, the headlines at 6 o'clock. Princess Margaret has had an operation at a hospital in London.
>
> More than twelve hundred miners have returned to work, the largest number to end their strike on any one day since November.

After the story about Princess Margaret, we hear the report on the miners which is mainly about the apparent return to work:

> (Newscaster) It's been the first full working day in the coal mines since the Christmas and New Year holiday and the Coal Board are claiming large numbers of miners took the opportunity to give up the strike. They say more men abandoned the strike today than on any day since the beginning of November.

The last sentence from the newscaster repeats the earlier headline. But we are now informed that the information on men returning is a claim from the Coal Board. From this we can see that a press release from the Coal Board has appeared as an unqualified statement in the news headlines. On local news programmes that night, the Coal Board's figures were attacked by the miners' leaders. Even in this bulletin we hear briefly that some of the coal industry management admit to being disappointed at how many have gone back. But the main emphasis in this BBC news is still on the big return to work:

> (Newscaster) Altogether twelve hundred miners were back at work despite wintry weather in some areas which made it hard to get to the collieries.
>
> The biggest returns were in the north-east, Yorkshire, and Scotland, which accounted for more than two-thirds of the new starters. We've reports from each of these areas starting in the north-east.

But in fact the BBC did not have just three reports from the north east, Yorkshire, and Scotland. They actually had reports from *four* areas. The fourth one is from Wales. Why did they

24 BBC1, 18.00, 7.1.85

miss it out from their introduction and from their graphic (Illustration 24)?

The theme of their story is the big return. With some trouble, the first three areas could be squeezed into this perspective. But the Welsh report creates a problem, since it shows that the return in South Wales was almost non-existent. So although this report is included in the news, it is not referenced in the above 'trailer'.

The news item continues with the reports from the four areas:

> (Reporter) Typical of the return in the north-east was Bates Pit at Blyth where twenty-nine men went back for the first time. They were, with sixty-six others already working, on two buses and this morning they almost outnumbered pickets. The increase here was prompted by a miner who placed an advertisement in a local newspaper.
>
> Elsewhere, miners were walking through picket lines for the first time. A total of almost 3,600 are back but the union says 18,000 are still out.

In the final sentence we hear at last from the union. The bulletin then moves on to the report from Yorkshire:

> (Reporter) The blanket of snow across the Yorkshire coalfields

helped explain the low turnout. Official pickets at Kellingly insisted it showed striker solidarity. In fact an extra 240 working miners braved the weather and the pickets' abuse – the highest daily figure in Yorkshire since last November. Twenty-nine new faces arrived at Kellingly and although disappointed the Coal Board management still say production will be resumed there later this week.

This report suggests that it is the weather which is preventing a larger return. In this it differs sharply from the views of those on strike who believe that the low numbers reflect union solidarity. There then follows the report from Scotland:

(Reporter) The Coal Board in Scotland hope for a big return to work but instead outside the threatened Polkemitt colliery they got a mass demonstration of fourteen Labour MPs among the pickets. The MPs denied that ten months into the strike their presence was too little too late. In all there are now 2,500 miners working in Scotland – the biggest return to work was in Ayrshire when 97 miners broke the strike at Killoch colliery.

This report from Scotland does not fit very well into the big return theme, though there is a clear attempt at it in the last paragraph. But the report from Wales offered an even more discordant note:

(Reporter) According to the Coal Board in South Wales more working miners than ever before turned up today – 141 of them. But according to the union the figure of 126 is the same as before Christmas. But which ever figure you believe the reality is that there has been no substantial return to work as forecast and the predictions of the Working Miners' Association that men would clock on at three new pits today have come to nothing.

(Newscaster) The Coal Board said its back-to-work figures were encouraging but the union said the anticipated surge back to work hadn't happened.

At last the two views appear together. But until this point the consistent emphasis has been on the Coal Board's perspective which was highlighted first in the news headlines. The underlying theme becomes the number of people who are returning rather than the number who have stayed out on strike.

But the bulletin does in fact contain a strong hint from one journalist that the return to work is being overplayed:

> (Reporter) The Coal Board has never said what size return to work constitutes a surge and what figure amounts to a flop – but nothing that has happened today has turned the course of the strike.

This was a routine news programme from two months before the end of the strike. Its story is told largely from the point of view of the government and the Coal Board. But this perspective does not follow necessarily from the information which it has to offer. The crucial issue is the way in which such information is shaped and then reproduced on the news. It is possible to tell a quite different story using the same 'facts'. We can illustrate this with an imaginary news written from a different perspective:

> (Newcaster) Good evening, the headlines at 6 o'clock.
>
> Princess Margaret has had an operation at a hospital in London.
>
> In the coal dispute, the anticipated surge back to work doesn't happen. That's according to the NUM, and some Coal Board management admit to being disappointed.
>
> It's been the first full working day in the coalmines since the Christmas and New Year holidays. There are mixed reports from the coalfields.
>
> In Wales, there was no substantial return to work as forecast. In Scotland there was a mass demonstration of Labour MPs among the pickets. In Yorkshire, just 240 extra miners went in and the management have expressed disappointment.
>
> In the fields of the north-east, the Coal Board is claiming that 3,600 miners are now back but the union says that 18,000 are still out. We've reports from all the four areas.

This 'news' uses the same information, but the underlying theme has changed from the persistent emphasis on how many people are returning.

Methodologies in content analysis

The Glasgow Media Group have argued in past research that content analysis can reveal the explanatory themes which underpin news accounts.[3] The present study suggests that there may be a clear correspondence between some themes as they are developed in the news and what is understood and remembered by the audience. Of course not all news offers a single, coherent way of interpreting events and not all audiences would accept the preferred interpretation. The news may offer contradictory accounts, or be confusing or simply irrelevant to the audience. But to the extent that the news is organized within specific ways of understanding, it is important to develop a methodology which reveals what these are.

The study by Cumberbatch, MacGregor, Brown, and Morrison (1986) of television news and the miners' strike raises some important issues in this area. It also illustrates some of the difficulties of moving from the analysis of news output to assumptions about audience beliefs. The content analysis in their study is based on counting the number of times that the various issues in the strike were raised in the news. Thus 'talks and negotiations' account for 15.6 per cent of total coverage, while issues of picketing and picketing violence account for 11.6 per cent. From this analysis, the authors wish to make statements about 'biases' in the news. There is a potential problem here since the authors do not situate all the different issues in the contexts in which they appear. 'Picketing violence' is a generic category into which is put references to dozens of different events. This makes it impossible to assess differences between news reports. For example, during the strike some news coverage of 'violence' in Kent differed sharply from coverage of picketing at Orgreave in Yorkshire. In Kent the BBC reported that there were violent struggles following the taking away of miners at random by the police:

> As policemen dragged individual miners from the crush, apparently at random, there were violent struggles.
>
> (BBC1, 21.00, 4.9.84)

By contrast, BBC reports about Orgreave on 18 June 1984 tended to blame the violence on the miners. We can see that the different arguments which surround these events are lost in a methodology which does not make a qualitative analysis of specific cases.

The authors make one foray into the area of qualitative analysis. They examine the television news coverage of Orgreave on 18 June and compare it with other evidence of the events of that day. This consists of a video made by the police themselves which appears to show that police actions triggered the violence.[4] From this they conclude that the BBC news coverage was 'one-sided' while that of ITN was a 'misrepresentation of what had happened'. They then make the surprising comment that:

> such biases in the news seem very infrequent and it is important to consider the overall pattern of coverage and not become bogged down in semiotic analysis of individual bulletins.
>
> (Cumberbatch *et al.*, 1986, p. 73)[5]

It is not clear on what basis they make such a statement, since this is the only case in which they look at alternative evidence and contrast what could have been said with what actually appeared on the news. In general, they eschew such a method, apparently regarding it as getting bogged down in semiotic analysis. This shows the suspicion which they have of methodologies which focus on how the news highlights and develops specific meanings. Instead they attempt to understand the 'overall pattern of coverage' by making the lists of issues which they abstract from the news. The importance of a given issue is assessed primarily by how many times it appears in news reports. The authors then attempt to relate their frequency count of the issues to the attitudes of the audience. These attitudes are assessed by using public opinion surveys of what is seen as 'most important'. For example, 'talks and negotiations' is the largest issue on the news, while 'pit closures' is at the top of their list of issues named by the public. From such data they conclude that television news has not set the agenda:

> If we assume that the number of times an issue appears on the news is a reasonable measure of the priority given to the issue, it is plain that the agenda of issues on the news did not match that as defined by the public although roughly the same issues were present for both. The evidence suggests, therefore, that

> television news did not 'set the agenda' of important issues for the public in any crude sense.
>
> (ibid., pp. 44–5)

This does show a very limited appreciation both of how television news establishes meanings and of its routine organizational practices. Television journalists are often obliged to cover events without necessarily believing that the story will be crucial. In the miners' strike, the news had to be present for each set of talks. They could not afford to miss the hypothetical moment when Scargill and MacGregor might emerge to announce a settlement. The talks were important for what they might produce, not for what actually took place. Once they failed, the news might then cue its audience into seeing the futility of the exercise. Consider the tone of this ITN comment on negotiations:

> The Coal Board and the miners' union took just under one hour to fall out again today . . .
>
> (ITN, 22.10, 23.5.84)

We have already heard how the BBC summarized the negotiations:

> Agreement remained as far away as ever – the TUC insisted on talks, once again they went badly.
>
> (BBC1, 21.10, 3.3.85, quoted above on p. 137)

Why would we expect an audience receiving such messages to believe that the long history of failed negotiations was of crucial importance? It is clearly not enough simply to count the issues which are named and make deductions based on the frequency of their appearance.

The problem for these authors arises because of their focus on the words that are used, rather than the meanings that are conveyed. Their analysis founders on the difficulties of removing words from the context in which they are understood. Martin Barker makes a similar point in his critique of the study:

> Content analysis of this kind assumed that the world falls into 'natural units', which can be counted; and meaning is added by interpretation afterwards.
>
> (1988, p. 109)

Barker highlights the problem of the potential differences

between 'coders' categories' and what the news actually means, both to those who produce it and to those who watch it. He comments on how 'personality clashes' is a major issue for the audience, but that it does not show up in the content categories given by Cumberbatch *et al.* The point is that the news might regularly present Scargill and MacGregor as being at loggerheads without actually using the words 'personality clashes'. But the audience might understand the news reports as being about this constant friction between the two men. This indicates the obvious point that the same meaning can be expressed in many different ways – either explicitly through different combinations of words, or perhaps implicitly through the structure of the coverage, for example by the persistent juxtaposition of conflicting comments from MacGregor and Scargill. Such subtleties are lost on the authors who reply to Barker that they did have a category for 'personalities', but that on television very few people 'mentioned this as an issue' (Cumberbatch *et al.*, 1988, p. 115).

They come near to acknowledging the problem with their method when discussing their attempt to identify 'significant verbs' in the news. In this part of their work, they tried to show how viewers might be encouraged to accept the truth of some viewpoints. They assume that the words used to introduce the views might be important. They comment that some verbs have a definite 'factual ring' about them, such as 'disclosed', 'stated', or 'reported', while others such as 'claimed' are more tendentious. They do not look at *what* is said to be claimed or stated, but only at the number of times the particular verb is used in relation to different actors. In the event, after counting a large number of decontextualized verbs, they acknowledge that it has shown very little:

> It is clear that no real support is offered from the above data for the hypothesis that differences would occur in the treatment of different actors on this measure. *Of course this statistical summary may disguise consistent differences* in the treatment of particular statements by particular actors but the task of unravelling results further would not seem merited. (my italics)
>
> (Cumberbatch *et al.*, 1986, p. 106)

Statistical summaries of this type certainly might disguise very many differences and shades of meaning. The problem is to find a method for assessing trends in coverage which does not violate such qualitative variations. Cumberbatch *et al.* are right to say that there must be a quantitative dimension to the analysis of news content. The problem is that the methodology which they have espoused counts words instead of meanings and makes it difficult for them to explain either what is being conveyed by the news or how it is being understood.[6]

The difficulties of linking a qualitative assessment of meaning with a quantative measure are well known. It is tempting for researchers to count the apparently 'hard' and discrete pieces of data which are most amenable to statistical analysis. Robert Frank, in his study of American television coverage, contrasts what he terms the 'hard' and 'soft' approaches:

> A major decision was whether to use the 'hard' or the 'soft' approach to content analysis, where the hard approach is defined as a simple frequency count of words, seconds or air-time coverage, and other discrete and concrete quantifiable bits of data. The 'soft' approach on the other hand, utilises the judgement of trained coders to evaluate the entire gestalt package of the news story, the news segment and/or even of the entire news broadcast.
>
> (Frank, 1973, p. 23)

But much of Frank's own research is taken up with the counting of phenomena which bear no direct relation to specific social meanings at all. For example, in his study of television news he counted the number and duration of graphics and 'voice over film' segments. Other dimensions of this type of analysis include counting the use of video as against film and the use of outside broadcast units and satellite transmissions. Some of the early work of the Glasgow University Media Group (1976) also involved efforts in this direction. Such analysis may tell us something about the allocation of technical resources to different stories, but tells us nothing of what was actually said or why these resources were so allocated.

These problems in the analysis of meaning are also highlighted in some of the attempts to assess news in terms of its 'bias' or neutrality. Here, the news is often dissected in order to count how often different people are reported or featured. Robert Frank's work included the measurement of the presence or absence of speakers for the administration and in his analysis of American elections he examined the amount of time given to candidates' statements and to general campaign coverage. But to count only 'who is reported' and 'how many times' says nothing of the function of statements in the flow of coverage and the organization of meaning. For example, when Gerald Ford was President, there was extensive coverage of the moment when he fell down a set of aircraft steps and, on another occasion, of him running from reporters as the Vietnam war ended. Later, the speeches and remarks of President Reagan became perhaps as well known for the mistakes which they contained as for their intended content. Yet it would be a rash media analyst who would code such stories as 'candidate coverage' and measure the time allocated for the purpose of assessing bias on the grounds of who had the most television exposure.

All of these problems turn on the relationship between the investigators' categories and the range and subtlety of meaning within actual news content. The difficulties exist whether the unit of analysis is the decontextualized word or a category such as 'candidate coverage' into which the data is grouped. The issue is not only that individual words change their meaning in use, but that the meaning of a whole message cannot be understood by reducing it to decontextualized fragments.[7]

Thematic analysis

The Media Group at Glasgow University developed an approach to content analysis which attempted to resolve some of these problems. A key issue was to show the meaning of individual words or statements in their specific contexts. But it was also clear that we had to understand how these contexts and the use of language within them related to wider social processes. We were interested in how differences in language and definitions related to conflict and divisions within the society as a whole. A crucial part of this analysis was to show how individual meanings and communications might be understood as being part of ways of understanding the nature and movement of the social world.

In our case study method, we saw the first task as to lay out these 'ways of understanding' and to relate them to the specific conflicts through which they were generated. In *More Bad News* (1980), we showed how divisions between right and left on the political spectrum corresponded to quite different explanations of the reasons for economic crisis. The language and definitions used were at one level the battle ground for competing groups. The issue is, then, not to look simply at the descriptions which are offered of the world but to look at the social relations which underpin the generation of the descriptions.[8] It seemed clear that different ways of explaining the world emerged from social divisions such as those between classes and between subgroups within these. Our interest was in examining how the key themes of social ideologies were represented in news accounts.[9]

In the event, we found in our research that the social relations which structure the wider society were referred to implicitly and explicitly in news reporting. A knowledge of these and what 'ought' to happen within them was assumed by the broadcasters and by those who supplied them with news. Such a world view involved assumptions of cause and responsibility which shaped the descriptions which were given. Obviously, not all information on the news was the subject of clearly competing viewpoints. Statements on the cause of an industrial dispute were more likely to be the subject of competing interpretations than a statement about what time the dispute started or which unions were involved.[10] Our main interest was in the treatment of themes on which there were manifestly different interpretations and in analysing how some of these dominated and gave direction to news accounts.[11]

There were three dimensions to this method of content analysis: firstly, the identification of the explanatory or interpretative themes; secondly, the examination of the manner in which each theme is developed in its specific context; thirdly, the assessment of the frequency with which different themes appear. The initial task is to identify the range of explanations which are current on an issue, such as what is thought to 'cause' inflation. In our study of this (1980) we identified all those which were present on the television news and in other sources such as newspapers and financial journals. From these we constructed what was in effect a 'map' of the different beliefs which were available in the political and economic debate of that time. Using this, we could then analyse how different parts of the debate were highlighted or developed in the news.[12]

In the first period of our research, in 1975, the alleged problem of high wage awards was very prominent in industrial and economic news. This was in a situation where many economists did not believe that wages were the source of inflation. Also by some indices real wages were actually static or falling. Nonetheless, the television news reported that:

> the problem facing the government is dealing with the inflationary pressure of wages.
>
> (BBC2, 22.30, 31.1.75)

Such diagnoses were linked to proposals for wage restraint as a solution to the economic crisis.

Our conclusion was that the organization of news reports was affected by assumptions on who was responsible for economic problems and how these might be solved. Although a variety of different opinions appeared in some form (and the illusion of balance was created) it was the case that some views had a special status in the coverage. These explanations were featured more frequently but in addition were highlighted in news headlines and summaries, and were directly embraced by media personnel. The key explanations were also underlined by linking them with other reported information, such as figures on wages and prices, and with 'official' reports. The structuring of interviews and the organization of questions similarly emphasized certain economic and political themes.

The dominant explanations had a further status in that their content was described exhaustively – indeed a large part of the coverage had the function of illustrating them. Some news was clearly organized within the logic and premises of these explanations. For example, in this *News Review* there is a remarkable combination of a narrow economic diagnosis and very debateable official figures, leading inexorably to the government's solution:

> Now home and as you know this week there has been a lot of heavy news on the country's economic front. Two figures from the week give the real story. Everything else in one way or another is a reaction to these figures.
>
> One: prices rose in the last twelve months by the biggest ever increase, 21 per cent.
>
> Two: Wages rose in the last twelve months by a far greater figure, 32 per cent.
>
> The Chancellor, Dennis Healey, for one, regards that extra 11 per cent on wages as the main cause of inflation. His

answer, as we saw in the budget on Tuesday, is to take the extra money away in taxes.

(BBC2, 18.15, 20.4.75)

At this time, these beliefs on the cause of inflation provided the rationale for a routine examination of the activities of trade unions in pursuing wage awards. The news felt free to comment on 'threats' and 'demands' from unions because it had established so firmly what the problem was. By contrast, alternative accounts appeared as fragments. News reports were not organized to illustrate the content of these alternatives or to follow through their meaning from their premises to their conclusions. When they did appear, they occurred in such a disparate form that their sense and rationality was lost.

Not all news is as 'closed' as this suggests. This is partly because journalistic assumptions about which explanations will dominate are overlaid by other beliefs and practices, such as the need to feature some form of apparent balance between views – if only at the level of interviewing opposing sides. The credibility of television news and the legitimacy which it seeks for itself depends upon its claim to be even-handed and 'fair' in controversal areas. Our research suggested that it is skewed in favour of the powerful, but the broadcasting institutions are intensely reluctant to be seen as simply the mouthpiece of the state.[13]

There is sometimes a real substance to their claims to be featuring a range of views. How 'balanced' they can be depends in part on the area of news. On issues where the state is very sensitive, such as in coverage of Northern Ireland, the news can become almost one-dimensional – alternatives are reduced to fragments or disappear altogether.[14]

But other conflicts such as the miners' strike of 1984/5 are defined more clearly as being within the boundaries of 'acceptable dissent'. Here, the broadcasters featured contrasting views and occasionally even made radical departures from traditional journalistic practice. For example, Channel 4 news gave Arthur Scargill and Ian MacGregor the opportunity to make their own short news items on the dispute, without normal editorial control.

But we also found that even where journalists are attempting to be even-handed, their underlying assumptions about the nature of the events can wield a powerful influence. In this example from the coverage of the miners' strike, the journalist acknowledges that there are two competing accounts about the origins of violence in a specific incident. Although we are told initially that there was 'violence on both sides' and that there are different views on its genesis, the events are described as the police being stoned followed by them 'responding' with baton charges:

> There then followed a pitched battle between police and pickets in a nearby housing estate. There were injuries, ten arrests, and for an hour the village was sealed off. There appears to have been violence on both sides – *the police were stoned and they responded* with baton charges, but *there were differing views about who started it.* (my italics)
>
> (BBC1, 21.00, 22.8.84)

In practice, our method revealed the 'preferred' meanings of the news. We showed how the repetition of certain views and explanations together with the embracing and underlining of them by journalists were part of a general process by which the news was structured. This was reflected in the choice of material, the themes that were emphasized, the links that were made between these, and the final conclusions that were drawn.

The importance of the current work is in showing how such key themes relate to processes of understanding and belief in audiences. The next section examines the implications of this work for contemporary debates on media 'effects'.

Issues in media effects

Much contemporary theory has downplayed the effectiveness of TV messages in persuading or informing audiences. I will look here at three main currents in this research. The first is the empirical study of people watching television and the study of the information which audiences absorb. This is best seen in the work of Peter Collett and Roger Lamb (1985) and Colin Berry and Brian Clifford (1986).

The second approach derives from empirical psychology and uses traditional survey techniques to assess the political attitudes of audiences, relating these to beliefs about the content of television news. One conclusion of these studies by Guy Cumberbatch *et al.* (1986) is that the perception of television messages is conditioned by the pre-existing political loyalties of the viewer (summarized in the phrase 'Bias is in the Eye of the Beholder').

The third area derives from the structuralist tradition and is seen in the work of communication researchers such as David Morley (1980 and 1986) and John Fiske (1987), who have focused attention on the uses to which messages are put by differently situated audiences.

The experiments by Collett and Lamb involved using a camera to make videos of people who were actually watching television. For some television professionals and academics, the results were quite 'startling'. In the words of Jane Root:

> The most startling thing about the resulting videos is the variety of ways in which we watch television. . . . People engage in an almost bizarre variety of different activities in front of the set: We eat dinner, knit jumpers, argue with each other, listen to music, read books, do our homework, kiss, write letters and vacuum clean the carpet.
>
> (1986, pp. 25–6)

Jane Root's book, entitled *Open the Box*, is based on a Channel 4 series of the same name. Peter Collett appeared on this and added his own comments about the implications of his study. He is clear that it indicates a reduction in the supposed power of television:

> One of the things that the material illustrates is that television is certainly not as powerful a medium as the producers of television programmes would lead us to suppose – in the sense that people will spend literally hours on end doing all kinds of things that have absolutely nothing to do with television viewing, while the set is on.
>
> (*Open the Box*, Channel 4, 19.5.86)

However, this does seem to be an unwarranted deduction by Collett from his own evidence. The lack of close attention might make television a more powerful medium in the communication of certain types or parts of messages, rather than a less powerful one. It might mean that messages which are highlighted, presented in a dramatic fashion, or persistently repeated are most likely to be retained by the audience. One of the women in my own study commented on the reasons why television news shows violent scenes. She believed that:

> They need to show you that or you would just carry on with what you were doing in the house. (quoted above on p. 97)

We might also consider the relation between dramatic news headlines and qualifications to these which may appear much later in the bulletin (and relatively *sotto voce* in terms of the presentational style of news). One example which we have already seen is the difference between a headline statement on the number of people who have returned to work in the miners' strike and the information given later that these figures are a *claim* by the Coal Board.

The work of Collett and Lamb does not add much to our knowledge of the relation between the perception of television and belief. What is most startling about the research is the surprise with which the findings were greeted by some television professionals and other experts. This is a point very astutely made by Joan Burnie, the television critic of the Scottish *Daily Record*. While reviewing the *Open the Box* series, she writes:

> It is altogether brain-boggling what can be learned from your telly these nights . . . did any of you out there know that when the set is switched on – and this is really going to leave you breathless – some of us actually DO OTHER THINGS.
>
> Yes, I bet that shook you rigid. You could have knocked me over with a video tape when they told me that.
>
> I mean, up until Channel 4 revealed all, I thought us TV viewers were chained to our chairs with padlocked peepers from Selina's first yawn on the breakfast couch until the late-night God slot.
>
> But no, as this programme, shock horror, informed us, at enormous expense, seriousness and length that while watching, some viewers have been known to fall asleep, lose interest, scratch, kiss the wife, kick the dog, move about, and even, oh heresy, ignore the set altogether.
>
> And this will give you the biggest surprise, . . . when the commercial breaks come on, many of us get up and make ourselves a fly cup of tea.
>
> Gosh and golly and may we be struck down for such a sin when they are telling us the delights of soap powder and supermarkets.
>
> But, as I said, it is absolutely amazing what the experts

come up with these days to rescue us from our slough of ignorance, and to educate us about our own lives.

Where would we all be without them?

(*Daily Record*, 23.5.86)

The knowledge that in 'ordinary' homes the television is frequently left on irrespective of other activities was treated by some as a major revelation. As Joan Burnie suggests, this perhaps says more about television professionals than about television audiences.

Learning from television news

The work of Colin Berry and Brian Clifford is an attempt to explain the role of presentational styles and other factors in determining how much information is absorbed from television news broadcasts. Their work has been linked with that of Peter Collett and Roger Lamb in that both pieces of research have been seen as indicating the ineffectiveness of television as a communication medium. Thus, Sue Summers writes in her review of the work that:

> The inescapable conclusion is that television has far less power over most of its viewers than is generally assumed.
>
> (*The Sunday Times*, 29.9.85)

Much of Berry and Clifford's work relates to the effect of different presentational styles in determining what viewers understand and retain from broadcast news. Thus they found that learning could be improved by reporting events in a clear narrative order. They also found that the alternating of male and female newscasters produced better learning than when the news was read by a single presenter (1986, p. 2). They conclude that such production variables are crucial and contrast this result with the findings of other theorists, such as Renckstorf, which have suggested that the interests of specific audiences are the key determinant of what is understood and retained.

In a further article, Colin Berry (1986) links his work on audience retention to debates about the impact of television on audience belief and to current arguments about 'bias' in television news. He writes that:

> It is disappointing to see another exchange of assertions about

> bias and news communications without reference to studies of the effects of broadcast messages.
>
> Yet there is now a considerable body of research on the communicational effectiveness of material such as TV and radio news and the factors that limit this effectiveness. Such research seems as yet little known among broadcasters. The evidence from both laboratory research and studies of audiences for live broadcasts, is sobering. People seem to be failing to grasp much of what it has been assumed is getting across. . . . My colleagues and I found, in work supported by the IBA, that knowledgeable, well-motivated grammar school sixth-formers retained little more than 60 per cent of the detailed news information they were tested on minutes after viewing.
>
> (1986, p. 30)

Colin Berry is clear about how much information is lost to the television viewers in his study. But there is also an important issue here in relation to what exactly is being *retained* by audiences.[15] My own research showed how different audience groups could reproduce key themes from coverage of the miners' strike. This was apparently so even where some people believed initially that the task was beyond them. We might remember that one of the women in the Bromley group had commented on her own lack of knowledge of the strike, saying:

> That shows how much television we watched. We used to turn it off, it was so boring.

But after the exercise was finished, she commented that:

> When you first asked me, I said I never watched it – then when you asked the questions I found it was amazing how much I remembered – how much you take in. (see p. 100)

How might we explain the apparent differences between the results of my study and that of Berry and Clifford? Firstly, we might note that there are some similarities. I found that many details of news coverage (times, dates, places, etc.) were not retained by the audience groups. But they could reproduce some of the key explanatory themes. This raises important issues in relation to what we as researchers are actually trying to measure. If we wish to understand the way in which people use the news to interpret their world then we might be better off employing a methodology which illustrates the explanatory frameworks of the news and how audiences relate to these, rather than simply noting the percentage of information which is forgotten. In this sense, one reason for the apparent difference in the results is that we are measuring different things in different ways.

Having said this, it is clear that Berry and Clifford did find a very high level of forgetfulness amongst their viewers. A further explanation for this might be the news topics which they picked for their tests. One of their most important examples utilized a news report on the assassination of the president of Korea in 1979. It does seem unlikely that the reporting of a single incident such as this would have the same impact on British audiences as the treatment by the news of an event such as the miners' strike. In the course of the strike a specific range of issues were presented and contested on the news night after night for a period of one year. We might expect the British audience's knowledge of these issues to be greater than their knowledge of Korea in 1979. They might also be expected to see the strike as a crucial political and industrial struggle which has implications for their own future. In the circumstances it is very likely that there would be variations in the retention and comprehension of information about the two issues.

It is important to analyse the process by which news information may be located within political perspectives which are promoted and contested in the development of social ideologies. Methods of analysing news comprehension are inadequate if they treat the content of news (events, places, causalities) as discrete units, irrespective of the processes by which the news is generated. It is not enough simply to assess how many of these different 'units' are retained in the memory. We can look, for example, at the study by Findahl and Höijer (1985) which involved testing groups of Swedish viewers on news memory after exposure to simulated news programmes. The news items were apparently selected randomly in terms of their significance to Swedish viewers (e.g. 'a ship aground' and 'a state of emergency in Peru'). The study concludes that information relating to places, persons, and things is more easily recalled than information on causes and consequences:

> . . . information about places and principals was more easily

> recalled than information about causes and consequences. . . . Our causal understanding of the world develops slowly,and causality can rarely be experienced in the same direct way as events, places, persons, and objects.
>
> (1985, p. 390)

However, my own study showed that not all 'causalities' have the same status in news text. Some are more vigorously contested than others. For example, there might be potential differences in the manner in which a British audience relates to an item on elections in Canada and to one on the miners' strike. Both items could contain statements about 'causes' but there is an essential difference between these two sets of causal explanations. This difference is likely to be in the manner in which they are contested in British society. In my study the rationale and the legitimacy of the miners' actions were central issues for the audience groups – not because these arguments constituted a specific type of information (i.e. 'causes' as opposed to 'places') but because of the social processes within which these knowledges were developed. In this sense studies of news memory might be improved if they attempt to situate both news and audience responses to it, in the social generation and promotion of meaning.

Bias in the eye of the beholder

The second general perspective to be examined here is the view that the perception of 'bias' in television is determined by the pre-existing political preferences of the viewer. It is developed most forcefully by Michael Tracey. In an article in the *Listener*, he writes that:

> Different people see the same thing in very different ways and for a variety of very different reasons. In that sense 'bias', like beauty, lies in the eye of the beholder; it is subjective as much as it is an objective condition.
>
> (*Listener*, 13.11.86, p. 8)

To support his argument, Tracey cites the study by Cumberbatch *et al.* (1986) on *Television and the Miners' Strike*, which has already been referred to above. This study included surveys of public opinion and Tracey quotes some of the results. He writes that:

> Labour voters were four times more likely than Conservatives to think the BBC biased against the miners, and seven times more likely to view ITN as biased. It is not difficult to explain this difference: only 4 per cent of Conservative voters were very sympathetic to the strike compared to 37 per cent of Labour voters. How one sees the news is therefore heavily influenced by one's attitude to the topic it is covering and, therefore, from this perspective no matter how television covers a given issue, accusations of bias are inevitable.
>
> (ibid.)

There are some problems with this analysis. Firstly, Tracey overstates the case which can be drawn from the work of Cumberbatch *et al.* He could have noted that this work also contains evidence that people may have a common perception of the news which traverses political beliefs. For example, the study showed that a majority of both Conservative and Labour voters saw television interviewers as being especially critical of Arthur Scargill. Writing in the *Guardian* (19.5.86), Cumberbatch notes this research finding but also comments on the view that 'bias is in the eye of the beholder'. His position is that while the perception of bias may not only be blamed on prejudice, the predispositions of viewers are nonetheless very important. As he writes:

> Our conclusions are that while 'bias' may be an inherent feature of the news, the explanation may not only be blamed on prejudice. Moreover, bias is very much in the eye of the beholder which raises some vital questions about the actual as opposed to the assumed role of television news in a political democracy.

In arriving at these conclusions, the methodology employed by Cumberbatch *et al.* was to use public opinion surveys of attitudes to the strike and television coverage of it, and then to relate these responses to voting intentions. In practice the researchers distinguished between people who would vote for the Labour party and those who would vote for the Conservative party 'if there were an election tomorrow' (1986, p. 15).

There is a problem here in that the study does not attempt to trace sources of beliefs about television coverage other than to relate them to political preference. But in my own work, I found regional differences between groups which were also conditioning their perception. For example, the regional press in the north was sometimes important as a source of alternative information. There were also differences between the north and south in terms of direct and indirect experience. No one in the southern groups worked alongside miners' wives or others who were closely involved in organizing the strike. No one in the southern groups had driven past miners' picket lines on the way to work and then compared what they had seen with the television images of the strike. We also saw how indirect contact with the events in the north could affect the beliefs of people in the south. One of the members of the Harlow group had a sister-in-law who lived in Nottingham and used information which she received from this relative to criticize the television images.

These examples indicate that living in the north was in itself a potential variable in the evaluation of television coverage. Now, as it happens Labour voters are much more predominant in the north than in the south. So the question is, do the measurements made by Cumberbatch *et al.* relate to political preference or to the availability of alternative experience and information which comes as a consequence of living in the north? Perhaps more probably, both sets of variables are operating to influence the evaluation of coverage. It seems to me that we can only resolve such puzzles by actually asking people about the sources of their information. It does not seem sufficient to rely on the measurement of variables which are established *a priori* by the investigator.

We can see similar difficulties in another of the major empirical examples offered by Cumberbatch *et al.* They make the assumption that the positioning of the cameras when filming tense or violent scenes may be important to viewers, in the sense that the camera angles might impart a sense of empathy to one side rather than another. They asked viewers whether they thought that news cameras were located behind police lines or behind the pickets. They report that more Labour voters than Conservatives judged the cameras to be behind the police lines and conclude that:

> it would seem reasonable to infer, therefore, that the higher sympathy for the miners amongst Labour voters is implicated in their selective memory for cameras being on the police 'side'

> of events. Similarly, lack of sympathy might have influenced Conservatives to remember the news selectively. . . .
>
> (1986, p. 27)[16]

The problem here is the assumption which they make about the source of memories – in the sense that they assume people are only remembering what they have seen on the news and that these recollections are only informed by political preference. During the strike, there was in fact an extensive public debate about the nature of television coverage. This was conducted in the miners' own publications, in the columns of the national press, and in television programmes such as Channel 4's *Right to Reply*. One specific argument which was raised related exactly to the question of the positioning of cameras at picket lines. For example, Gus MacDonald from *Right to Reply* interviewed the industrial correspondents of BBC and ITN. He asked them:

> Is it not the case that if you get police and pickets together, your cameras are nearly always behind the police looking at the angry pickets and very seldom in amongst the miners looking at the police?

One of the correspondents, Martin Adeney, agrees and comments that:

> I must say I tend to agree with you. I spoke to some of our reporters today who had just come back from a picket line and I said, 'how often do you go behind the miners' side?' They said 'very rarely, because you have trouble if you do. You get jostled if you do to say the least'.
>
> (*Right to Reply*, 1.6.84)

Now according to the findings of Cumberbatch *et al.*, Labour voters were distinctly more interested in the strike than Conservatives and were apparently more likely to increase the amount of news which they watched (1986, p. 15). In these circumstances, it does seem quite possible that the views of Labour voters reflect a greater exposure to the arguments about television coverage and to the views of journalists such as Martin Adeney rather than a selective perception of specific news items. Here again, we face the problem of the sources of belief.

There is another sense in which this problem is crucial. The method employed by Cumberbatch *et al.* offers an immediate snapshot of the relation between beliefs and political preferences at a given moment. In this sense their model is static. The problem is that political beliefs do not remain inviolate and unchangeable within the population as a whole. They may alter over time in relation to new conditions and perhaps in relation to new information. The question is, under what conditions do they change and what is the role of the media in reinforcing or undermining key elements of belief?

The issues raised by the work of Cumberbatch *et al.* are developed more fully by the next group of theorists who are attempting to develop a general approach to the relation between social structure and processes of 'decoding' by audiences.

Socially situated audiences

The third general perspective attempts to show how audience perceptions and reactions to television will vary between differently situated groups. It is best seen in the work of David Morley, who analysed responses to a popular news/current affairs programme called *Nationwide* which at one time had a regular evening slot on BBC television. He chose two programmes from 1976 and 1977 and showed them to groups of people with different backgrounds (trade unionists, bank managers, etc.). After each showing, he initiated a group discussion which was then used as his basic research data.

In his work, Morley attempts to link the different interpretations which the groups make of the programmes back to socio-economic structures. His project is to show how members of different cultural groups and classes share different 'codes' and 'competencies' and how these affect or 'determine' the decoding of messages. He cites Voloshinov (1973) to argue that consciousness is essentially a social product and is developed 'only in the process of social interaction' (Morley, 1980, p. 14). Differences in class and cultural experience may potentially produce differences in social consciousness, and these will affect the interpretations which are made of the dominant ideological perspective.

Morley's argument is that if such potential differences in interpretations exist, then the meaning of a programme to the audience cannot be deduced simply by analysing the text itself. As he comments:

> to raise this as a problem for research is already to argue that the meaning produced by the encounter of text and subject cannot be 'read off' straight from textual characteristics.
>
> (1980, p. 18)

His view is that critical research must focus on the 'use' to which a text is put. He quotes Neale as arguing that:

> what has to be identified is the use to which a particular text is put, its function within a particular conjuncture, in particular institutional spaces, and in relation to particular audiences.
>
> (Neale, 1977, pp. 39–40)

But Morley does not wish to pursue these 'uses' at an individual level. He sees such an approach as psychologistic and reminiscent of the 'uses and gratifications' model, from which he is seeking to make a decisive break. His concern is with the subject's position in the social formation and how this:

> . . . structures his or her range of access to various discourses and ideological codes, and [how] correspondingly different readings of programmes will be made by subjects 'inhabiting' these different discourses.
>
> (1980, p. 158)

In developing this approach he utilizes a theory of ideology which is strongly influenced by the work of Louis Althusser. The key concept is that of the 'ideological problematic', which is in effect a structure of thought which sets limits on what can be understood and on what questions can be addressed.[17] For example, such a theory might imply that people organized in trade unions can develop only a 'limited' critique of the capitalist order, focusing on inequality and the struggle over wages and conditions. The implication is that to move beyond such a critique would require the science of Marxism.

One of the assumptions which is derived from this approach is that the problematic defines an agenda of issues which are 'visible' or 'invisible'. As Morley writes:

> The concept 'ideological problematic' designates not a set of 'contents' but rather a defined space of operation, the way a problematic selects from, conceives and organises its field of reference. This then constitutes a particular agenda of issues which are visible or invisible, or a repetoire of questions which

> are asked or not asked. The problematic is importantly defined in the negative – as those questions or issues which cannot (easily) be put within a particular problematic – and in the positive as that set of questions or issues which constitute the dominant or preferred 'themes' of a programme.
>
> (1980, p. 139)

But the problematic within which the programme *Nationwide* is constructed does not necessarily correspond with the problematics occupied by its audience. This is in fact the essence of Morley's case:

> We must not assume that the dominant ideological meanings presented through television programmes have immediate and necessary effects on the audience. For some sections of the audience the codes and meanings of the programme will correspond more or less closely to those which they already inhabit in their various institutional political, cultural and educational engagements, and for these sections of the audience the dominant readings encoded in the programme may well 'fit' and be accepted. For other sections of the audience the meanings and definitions encoded in a programme like *Nationwide* will jar to a greater or lesser extent with those produced by other institutions and discourses in which they are involved – trade unions or 'deviant' subcultures for example – and as a result the dominant meanings will be 'negotiated' or resisted.
>
> (1980, p. 159)

There may, however, be a correspondence between the television problematic and that of a particular audience group. Morley argues that such people will see the television account as being simply common sense – and crucially, the alternatives which television has excluded will be 'invisible' to them. Thus, he assumes that when a group of people who are politically conservative watch an edition of *Nationwide* which embodies 'their' way of understanding the economy, they will not be aware of the programme's 'problematic'. He refers to 'an invisibility produced by the equivalence between the group's problematic and that of the programme. . . .' (1980, p. 144)

There are some problems with this analysis. The first is in the manner in which he derives his evidence for this argument. Morley develops a theory advanced by Ian Connell that a key indicator is 'the absence of any spontaneous comment about the discourse as such' (Connell, 1978). Thus in his own work, Morley argues that 'this lack of comment is evidence of the invisibility' of the programme's problematic to the conservative groups (1980, p. 144).

However, it does not seem legitimate to equate a lack of comment with a lack of *awareness* that there are a range of positions on the economy and on how it could and should work. It may be the case that people are motivated more to comment on programmes with which they disagree than those of which they approve. Morley does not demonstrate that the alternatives *are* invisible. To do so would require asking the groups to construct an alternative and then analysing what they are able to produce.

A further problem with Morley's analysis is that his own evidence shows examples of both conservative and radical groups who are clearly aware of alternative positions on the economy. In one case, a group of bank managers who are politically conservative actually criticized *Nationwide* for promoting the conservative position without giving what they see as a proper 'balance' of views. In Morley's terms they are able to 'deconstruct' the programme. In this instance, the edition of *Nationwide* included an interview with an accountant who was presented as a neutral commentator. In the event this 'expert' gives a very conservative view of economic policy, focusing on the need for tax cuts to provide incentives and the need for cuts in public expenditure. The group of bank managers who watch this comment that:

> Particularly that accountant from Birmingham . . . was . . . very much taking a view very strongly, that normally would only be expressed with someone else on the other side of the table. . . .
>
> (1980, p. 106)

Morley, in fact, found many examples of audiences being able to de-construct the programmes by 'seeing through' loaded questions etc. But this ability to deconstruct did not necessarily mean that the audience members rejected the view that was being promoted. This was contrary to Morley's own expectations. With his characteristic frankness, he acknowledges the tension between what he expected to find and his own empirical observations:

> When I began the research I expected to find a clear division so that de-coding practices would either be unconscious (not recognising the mechanisms of construction of preferred readings) and as such, in line with the dominant code or else, if conscious, they could recognise the construction of preferred readings and reject them. In fact, the recognition of 'preferring' mechanisms is widespread in the groups and combines with either acceptance or rejection of the encoded preferred reading; the awareness of the construction by no means entails the rejection of what is constructed.
>
> (1980, p. 140)

As we have already seen, my own study contains many examples of people who clearly do not occupy a discrete conceptual space which renders invisible all other ways of thought. Individuals may be aware of, or partly share, elements of a range of ideological positions (or class-linked perspectives). There are at least two reasons for this. Firstly, the beliefs of an individual are not a single coherent entity derived in a linear fashion from one aspect of their class position. Many different levels of social experience may follow from our gender, class, culture, and history. These may produce contradictory elements within our beliefs. David Morley acknowledges this in his more recent work. He comments in *Family Television* (1986) on the assumptions which underpinned his *Nationwide* studies:

> This is to stress the point that the Althusserian drift of much early cultural studies work (and it is this which, evidently, underlies much of the *Nationwide* project) would reduce [a shop steward] to the status of a mere personification of a given structure, 'spoken' by the discourses which cross the space of his subjectivity. . . .
>
> Crudely, this is to argue that there is a tendency in the *Nationwide* book to think of deep structures (for instance, class positions) as generating direct effects on the level of cultural practice. That is a tendency which I would want to qualify more now, to examine in detail the different ways in which a given 'deep structure' works itself out in particular contexts, and to try to reinstate the notion of persons actively engaging in cultural practice.
>
> (1986, p. 43)

To illustrate how different levels of experience may affect the 'decoding' of a programme, Morley constructs a set of hypothetical reactions from a white male shop steward who he presents as watching a 'typical' edition of *Nationwide*. He imagines the person to be watching at home, away from the strong group values of his work-place:

> So, his working class position has led him to be involved in trade union discourses and thus despite the weaker frame supplied by the domestic context, he may well still produce an oppositional reading of the first item – on the latest round of redundancies. However, his working class position has also tied him to a particular form of housing in the inner city, which has, since the war, been transformed before his eyes culturally by Asian immigrants, and the National Front come closest to expressing his local chauvinist fears about the transformation of 'his' area: so he is inclined to racism when he hears on the news of black youth street crimes – that is to say, he is getting close to a dominant reading at this point. But then again his own experience of life in an inner city area inclines him to believe the police are no angels. So when the next item on the programme turns out to be on the Brixton riots he produces a negotiated reading, suspicious both of black youths and also of the police. By now he tires of *Nationwide*, and switches over to a situation comedy in which the man and woman occupy traditional positions, and his insertion within a working class culture of masculinity inclines him to make a dominant reading of the programme. . . .
>
> So, we have here a person making different readings of the same material in different contexts, and making different readings of material on different topics – oppositional in some areas, dominant in others.
>
> (1986, pp. 42–3)

There is a second reason why we should not understand the social individual as being 'sealed off' in a specific point of view which represents a fixed class position. Individual beliefs exist in the context of wider social and political arguments. Parties, class fractions, and interest groups contest how the world is to be explained and what is to be understood as necessary, possible, and desirable within it. They struggle for the consent of key sections of classes and groups within their society. In doing so they attack the weaknesses of each other's positions and tacitly acknowledge each other's strengths. In the course of political struggles we may speak of the dominant currents of thought as 'moving' to the right or to the left. In our own recent history we can see a series of decisive changes where the consent of a large part of the population has been won for some elements of a political ideology. When Conservative politicians declare, for example, that 'the health service is safe in our hands', it is not because they wish voluntarily to abandon free market principles in this area. Such a statement is a tacit acknowledgement of the strength of the political victory for social principles in health care which has been won in the past and which Conservative politicians are reluctant to challenge (at least in their public statements).

The reaction of the individual to such ideologies is thus likely to be constantly in flux. This is because of the potential contradictions within his or her own social experience and because the ideologies are themselves constantly subject to being reworked in relation to new economic and political circumstances and in the attempt to mobilize consent within the society (although there clearly are elements which are fundamental to ideologies such as the need to achieve or sustain class power and to base this on the maintenance of a specific economic system).[18]

A key issue in analysing the media in relation to social ideologies is their role in reflecting or developing key elements of belief about how the social world actually works and what is occurring within it. It may be crucial to know whether most picket lines *are* actually violent most of the time, or whether there *are* actually less places available in public hospitals since a particular government came to power. The 'facts' which we are given on the news and how such information is negotiated are crucial moments in the development of wider systems of belief.[19]

David Morley's work is an important contribution to this area, but he could have developed it further in the direction of examining the constituent elements of belief systems and in tracing their origins. There are moments in the *Nationwide* study (1980), where his interviewees make comments which are potentially very revealing. One of the items in the programme which they watch relates to six car workers who have won £600,000 on the football pools. The item includes a shot of the workers outside their factory. As soon as this picture is shown, several groups interpret the item as being about a strike. One person comments that the:

> First thing you think, whenever you hear of British Leyland is 'Who's on strike this time?'
>
> (Morley, 1980, p. 46)

Morley has important evidence on audience beliefs in this area but does not develop it by asking his groups about the sources of their information and the conditions under which they believe news accounts. He leaves his analysis in this area at the level of an assertion about possible media effects. He comments on one group's response to the car workers item that:

> Their decoding of this item is informed by, and leads into a generalised exposition of, a stereotype of the 'greedy car worker/mindless union militants' presumably derived, at least in part, from the media.
>
> (1980, p. 127)

Overall, Morley is agnostic on the question of effects. His focus is on the manner in which subgroups use messages – on 'negotiations' and on 'cultural competence'. He is unhappy with traditional effects studies inasmuch as they are based on a crude stimulus-response model which cannot grasp the complexity of the decoding process. But in my view, the derivation of frameworks of meaning, the sources which people use for information, and the conditions under which we accept what we are told are all crucial questions. Morley is right to argue that the complexities of cultural meanings and ideologies cannot be reduced to a simple set of yes/no answers on what programmes people have seen and which way they vote. But because we reject such methods it does not follow that the source of ideologies and their impact is of no interest to us. We must address the social processes by which meanings are generated, promoted, and contested. The political culture of society is the site of a struggle in which meanings are purposefully constructed. Phrases such as 'one-sided disarmament', 'the winter of discontent', 'inflationary wage demands', and 'popular capitalism' do not simply evolve independently of human action. They are thought up and *used* in response to specific situations and conflicts. In focusing on the decodings of such messages by subgroups we must not lose sight of the struggle to establish and legitimize meanings as the 'everyday common sense' that Morley is investigating. We must not remove from the debate the question of which interests have the most power to influence and direct the flow of information and whether such control actually makes any difference to the way in which key relationships in our society are explained and understood.

In his later work Morley moves further away from the analysis of the origins of belief and focuses instead on how television is watched within family contexts. Not surprisingly, he finds the practice of television watching to be influenced by the social relations within which it is situated. Male dominance in the family is reflected in control over the choice of programmes (and of course the automatic channel changer). This work has some interest but does not relate very directly to the role of television in the development of specific belief systems. Much of his analysis would apply equally to the use of other household objects such as the 'family' car (which might end up being driven most by the husband/father). But overall Morley's work is important not least because he insists on the need for empirical investigation. As he writes:

> Crucially, we are led to pose the relation of text and subject as an empirical question to be investigated, rather than as an a priori question to be deduced from a theory of the ideal spectator 'inscribed' in the text. . . . The relation of an audience to the ideological operations of television remains in principal an empirical question: the challenge is the attempt to develop appropriate methods of empirical investigation of that relation.
>
> (1980, p. 162)

The strength of Morley's work is that he takes his hypotheses on the ideological operations of television out to the world of talking, acting, believing subjects, and contends with the problems of relating our neat theoretical systems to the real society. It is ironic that some theorists, such as John Fiske, who have sought to commend and develop Morley's work have themselves lost contact with many of the processes by which audiences come to understand their world.

Audiences and 'television culture'

A number of theorists have recently begun to re-evaluate the relation between audiences and television. Morley's work is well known in this area, but others such as Hodge and Tripp (1986) have focused on the 'active' role of audiences and have argued for the primacy of social relations in the development of 'readings' of television. Fiske brings together several of these strands of thought in his *Television Culture* (1987a) and in his work on discourse theory (1987b).

In his analysis, Fiske makes the crucial assumption that the television text is polysemic. That is:

> The television text is a potential of meanings capable of being used with a variety of modes of attention by a variety of viewers. To be popular then, television must be both polysemic and flexible.
>
> (1987a, p. 84)

He cites a variety of textual characteristics which may 'open up' the text to polysemic readings. These include irony, contradiction and 'excess'. For example, a series such as *Dynasty* contains characters who operate in such an exaggerated fashion that the programme may be seen by some as a parody. Thus he quotes Schiff (1985) as showing how *Dynasty* has become a cult show amongst gays in the USA.

Following Barthes (1975), Fiske speaks of 'the writerly text' which requires us, the readers:

> to participate in the production of meaning and thus of our own subjectivities, it requires us to speak rather than be spoken to and to subordinate the moment of production to the moment of reception.
>
> (1987a, p. 95)[20]

We might note in passing that the results of my own study showed that the different groups had a relatively uniform understanding of what the television message had been on violence during the miners' strike and on who was portrayed as being responsible for it. As we saw, the message was at times renegotiated but this took the form of arguing that the news had concentrated on violence by miners and had *not shown* the other side of the story. There was very little ambivalence over what the intended message actually consisted of, although there were clear differences between groups over whether it was believed.

However, we can pass on the second major element in Fiske's approach, which is how texts are 'read' by differently situated social audiences. As he writes:

> Textual studies of television now have to stop treating it as a closed text, that is, as one where the dominant ideology exerts considerable, if not total, influence over its ideological structure and therefore over its reader. Analysis has to pay less attention to the textual strategies of preference or closure and more to the gaps and spaces that open television up to meanings not preferred by the textual structure, but that result from the social experience of the reader.
>
> (1987a, p. 64)

This stage of his analysis is concerned with how meanings are determined socially. He believes that the value of the approach developed by theorists such as Morley (1980) and Hall (1980) is that it moves away from the text and towards the reader as the site of meaning. As he writes:

> Meanings are determined socially: that is, they are constructed out of the conjuncture of the text with the socially situated reader.
>
> (1987a, p. 80)

He shares with Morley an interest in how the differently situated groups may produce different readings of a text – thus he speaks of a 'working-class reading' or a 'feminine reading' (1987a, p. 81), and he argues that:

> The reader produces meanings that derive from the intersection of his/her social history with the social forces structured into the text.
>
> (1987a, p. 82)

We might recall that Morley acknowledged the possibility that the meanings brought to a new text might derive from earlier contacts with the media. Fiske, by contrast, moves towards the position adopted by Hodge and Tripp that the subcultural meanings brought to television by its audiences overwhelm those of the text itself. He quotes from Hodge and Tripp's (1986) conclusions, that their studies:

> constitute a compelling argument for the primacy of general social relations in developing a reading of television rather than the other way about

and that:

> we must be prepared to find that non-television meanings are powerful enough to swamp television meanings.
>
> (quoted in Fiske, 1987a, p. 83)

These non-television meanings derive from the 'discourse of the reader'. By a discourse Fiske means a language or system of representation that has developed socially in order to make and circulate a coherent set of meanings, which serve the interests of a section of society (1987a, p. 14). Fiske pursues the argument that reality itself is only accessible to us through the discourses which we have available to make sense of it. He quotes his own earlier work with O'Sullivan and others (1983) in which reality is defined as a product of discourse:

> When O'Sullivan *et al.* (1983) define reality as a product of discourse they are, albeit somewhat mischievously, contradicting head-on the belief in an objective reality, accessible to all on equal terms and representable objectively or transparently.
>
> (1987a, p. 41)

A corollary of this for Fiske appears to be that the only way of evaluating a text is from within the boundaries of a specific discourse. They are, therefore, no 'general' criteria which could be applied to a text, such as whether a news item is 'accurate'. As he writes:

> Arguments that news should be more accurate or objective are actually arguments in favour of news's authority, and are ones that seek to increase its control under the disguise of improving its quality. News, of course, can never give a full, accurate, objective picture of reality nor should it attempt to, for such an enterprise can only serve to increase its authority and decrease people's opportunity to 'argue' with it, to negotiate with it.
>
> (1987a, p. 307)

For Fiske, there is little difference between news and fiction:

> the differences between news and fiction are only ones of

> modality. Both are discursive means of making meanings of social relations and it is important that readers treat news texts with the same freedom and irreverance that they do fictional ones.
>
> (1987a, p. 308)

In Fiske's view, arguments for accuracy in the news are also reactionary. They are used by men in the family to legitimize watching the news, which itself is designated by Fiske as having a 'masculine narrative form'. By contrast, women prefer soap opera, described by Fiske as having a feminine form, which opens it up to 'strategies of resistance'. He tells us that in this structure of the soap opera:

> All sides of an issue can be explored and evaluated from a variety of social points of view, and, in contrast to the masculine narrative . . . no point of view, no evaluative norm, is given clear hierarchical precedence over any other.
>
> (1987a, p. 195)

The news, by contrast, asserts 'a masculine closure and sense of achievement'. Even worse, it is preferred by men and used by them to assert the superiority of their tastes in programming:

> The male's preference for news, documentary, sport, and realistic 'muscle' drama becomes translated into the 'natural' superiority of these genres, which, in turn, allows the male to impose his viewing tastes upon the household, not because he is more powerful, but because the programmes he prefers are innately 'better'.
>
> (1987a, p. 76)

Consequently, according to Fiske we should assert the essential fictionality of news. As he writes:

> A wider and more self-confident recognition of this essential fictionality of news might lead its masculine viewers to treat its texts with the same socially motivated creativity as do the feminine viewers of soap operas.
>
> (1987a, p. 308)

I disagree with most of this. Firstly, while it is clear that we make sense of our world via frameworks of meaning and language, it is not the case that perceptions of this 'reality' are confined exclusively within the boundaries of a given subculture. Fiske's view of the real and of our perceptions of what is accurate neglects the problem of 'outcomes'. The perceived outcomes of our relationships, beliefs, and actions in the world can be acknowledged within the political/cultural assumptions of various groups. In this sense a range of 'discourses' can share common elements. For example, let us consider the difference between a window and a door. Now to one person from a specific subgroup, the window may have connotations of the surreal, perhaps of Magritte paintings, and the door may symbolize the relation between the inner and outer self. But to another person from a different subgroup the window may be simply somewhere to hang his National Front poster and the door is the obvious place for the dart board. Yet the members of both subgroups understand key differences between a window and a door because a failure to distinguish between them has a clear impact on their lives (should they live six floors up and leave by the wrong one, for example).

But Fiske writes as if the only distinctions made in the social world are those informed by the cultural assumptions of subgroups. Thus the distinction between fact and fiction on television comes down simply to the preferences of men and women for different types of programming, such as news versus soap operas.[21]

While we can accept that our experience in the social world makes sense to us via language and culture, it does not follow that differences in cultural codes pre-empt the possibility of any mutually agreed information or the acceptance of 'accuracy' as a desirable property. We can illustrate this with another analogy between male preference for news and male preference for car maintenance as domestic activities. We might see that 'going to work on the car' has all sorts of masculine connotations and resonances within our culture. These may not be shared and indeed may be clearly rejected by a 'feminine' culture. But both men and women may have a vested interest in the precision of a vehicle's steering and brakes and recognize the outcome of a failure in these areas. How far would we travel with Fiske's argument (or in his car) were he to claim that the masculine connotations of car mechanics mean that we should abandon all concern with accurate car maintenance?

The manner in which sections of the media conduct themselves in relation to criteria such as 'accuracy' and 'balance' can also have real outcomes in terms of how audiences perceive them. For example, in Britain the popular press has a very low level of public credibility, which contrasts with a much higher level of trust in television news as a source of information. We might argue that this is in part related to the 'style' of television news which avoids overt editorializing and seeks to be more authoritative in its presentation than the tabloids. But audience evaluations can also relate to the history and specific actions of the different media. For example, the assessment of a popular paper as an information source might be conditioned by its history of producing stories which are inaccurate or simply invented. If a newspaper publishes false information and is caught (i.e. is exposed/has to pay damages/publish an apology etc.) then this may undermine its credibility as a source, even with those who happen to identify with its political and cultural perspectives. The point is that there are potential differences between news sources to which audiences can respond, in ways that are not solely dependent on the readers' location in a particular subculture.

If we look for a moment at the content of three different items of news, we can see how measurable differences between them emerge. News accounts offer perspectives and exist within specific ways of understanding the world, but it does not follow that they all have an equal claim to accuracy. Let's consider first, the MYSTERY OF ELTON'S SILENT DOGS. This was a front page story in the *Sun* newspaper, billed as 'another *Sun* exclusive'. In this report, 'two vicious Rottweiler dogs' supposedly owned by Elton John were said to have been silenced by 'a horrific operation to stop them barking'. The paper claimed that:

> furious RSPCA chiefs immediately launched a probe and branded the operation 'evil and outrageous'.
>
> A spokesman said: 'Who knows what sort of suffering this will cause to these dogs?'

The story continued with the details on where the dogs had been sighted:

> The two *owned by Elton* were seen with security men in the 37-acre grounds of his fortress-style mansion near the Queen's estate at Windsor, Berks. (my italics)
>
> (*Sun*, 28.9.87)

The next day, it was revealed that Elton John did not own any Rottweiler dogs. The *Sun* printed his statement and claimed in its own defence that 'we never said Elton John owned the Rottweilers' (29.9.87). But in the edition of the paper quoted above, they had very clearly done so.[22]

We can compare this with a second example which is from a BBC news bulletin on the miners' strike, already quoted on p. 158:

> More than twelve hundred miners have returned to work, the largest number to end their strike on any one day since November.
>
> (BBC, 7.1.85)

We might well criticize this report but not on the same grounds as the previous one from the *Sun*. We would not state that it is simply untrue since there was some return to work (albeit there were disagreements over exactly how many people this involved). We might argue, however, that the report was *partial*. This is in the sense that it represents the Coal Board's perspective, by focusing on the return to work rather than on the number of people who were still on strike. We have also seen in the earlier analysis of this news how some information which weakened the Coal Board case was downplayed or neglected – for example the disappointment expressed by management about the numbers who had returned. There is thus the potential for an argument about the 'balance' of such items, and the manner in which different views have been represented.

We can engage in such an argument in the knowledge that there is no perfect 'balanced account' with which everyone will finally agree. But the difference between how the news actually reports and what it could have included always provides the terrain for a cultural struggle. This is a struggle in which journalists themselves have sometimes taken an active role, in the sense that they have seriously questioned what should be offered by a public service broadcasting which is committed to balance and impartiality. They have utilized the concept of balance to break the normal rules on who are 'acceptable' speakers and what are the 'legitimate' points of view which can be developed on the news. In British television this can be most clearly seen in the controversies which have frequently broken out over coverage of Northern Ireland. Some journalists have also at times questioned other routine practices of news production and the typical images of the world which are offered. The third item of news which is included here gives some indication of this struggle within television. It is a commentary from BBC2's *Newsnight* on a visit to West Germany by President Reagan. It is notable both for the forthright criticisms of the visit which it features and for the general critique which it offers of such media events:

> So here Mr Reagan is, undeniably the least widely admired President ever to tread on German soil – but determined to make a good impression on the people who once were proud to be called 'America's most uncritical friends in Europe'.
>
> Years ago, American Presidents used to move among the people in these European tours but that has become too dangerous. There are no crowds on this trip; to catch a glimpse of their American visitor, Germans must turn to television with its narrow view of a few carefully controlled events and non-events like arrivals and departures of the glamorous and the great.
>
> (BBC2, 23.00, 9.6.82)

How then do we distinguish between these three examples of news? We have one of a story which is apparently false, another which develops a partisan position, and a third which attempts to deconstruct the priorities of news production. Are they all to be simply grouped into the category of 'masculine soap opera'? It is my view that difference in the evaluation of such items may not be reduced purely to the uses to which the news is put in the family. Audiences as well as academics can apply evaluative criteria which relate to questions such as accuracy, coherence, and contradiction. A concern with these may cut across the various cultural competencies of given subgroups. In the BBC2 programme quoted above, the journalist reveals some of the criteria by which audiences in Germany could evaluate the contradictions in Reagan's position on arms control:

> President Reagan's cultivation of his European allies has been well prepared in a series of speeches and political moves towards arms control. These have been received here with relief, but to many Germans his conversion from rearmer to disarmer has been too sudden and too slick to be convincing. There was a vivid example of President Reagan's over-anxiety to please in his speech today to the Bunderstadt – the lower

> house of the German parliament. There, he came close to aligning himself to a German peace movement which only four months ago he was condemning as led and financed by the Kremlin.
>
> (BBC2, 23.00, 9.6.82)

If there was indeed a major shift in the perception of Reagan, then we might ask, why? Was it because there had been a major shift in the composition of subcultures in Germany and therefore he was seen differently; or was it the nature of Reagan's conduct which resulted in him losing credibility with many different groups?[23]

To be caught in contradiction and confusion can be disastrous for politicians. We might consider the difficulties of the British Labour Party during the 1983 General Election, notably in relation to its defence policy. In this case, two different sections of the party were offering contradictory versions of the meaning of its commitment to unilateralism. One argued that nuclear armaments would be abolished immediately on taking power, the other that the arms would be retained to 'bargain' for corresponding cuts by the Soviet Union. In this situation policy statements dissolved into confusion, and echoes of these arguments dogged the Labour Party through to the next election in 1987. During this, the case was very strongly made by the party's opponents that the Labour leader was trying to avoid the issue of defence altogether. In practice, politicians and others who provide key inputs to the media frequently acknowledge the strengths and weaknesses of their own arguments, by seeking to highlight issues where they feel they are strong and by avoiding the 'difficult' areas. This involves the tacit acknowledgement of the strength of other positions, albeit that politicians will rarely admit openly that the evidence and arguments of the 'other side' are superior to their own.

We must also acknowledge that people who are arguing from different perspectives frequently contest the legitimacy or relevance of each other's evidence.[24] Nonetheless, we do not all remain inviolable within our preconceptions and expectations. The key role of television news is as a relatively legitimate provider of information about what has apparently occurred in the world. As audiences, we have then to decide how this information relates to these expectations and values, and crucially whether the news account can be integrated into our beliefs or if it is to be dismissed as false, partial, or simply irrelevant. As communication researchers we have to understand both the manner in which the media provide some elements of how the world is understood and the process by which its messages are interpreted, believed, or rejected.

The evidence of my own study was that some audience members did use direct experience or logical processes to reject news accounts and they could at times do so apparently independently of their own prior commitments on the issues involved. By contrast, we might also remember that there were many people in the groups who depended on television news as their main source of information and that the television account of the nature of picketing in the strike was very widely accepted. In terms of the impact of subcultural values, the evidence was that some people who were sympathetic to the striking miners still accepted the news account on issues such as the nature of picketing (and were consequently depressed by what they came to believe); while some others who were *not* sympathetic to the miners were critical of what they saw and heard on the news (using logic, experience, or general beliefs about news values). Having said this, there is no doubt that there were also cases where the news message was re-negotiated or completely rejected via the subcultural beliefs of groups such as the Scottish trade unionists, the print workers, and of course the miners themselves. John Fiske would certainly recognize this dimension to the relationship between television and its audiences. My objection to his work is that he sees the processes by which news is evaluated as being located only in the codes and competencies of relatively discrete subcultures and tends to assume that these are likely to overwhelm television messages. The meaning, accuracy, and balance of accounts can thus only be understood in relation to subcultural usage. This leads us to a form of relativism in which there is ultimately no difference between any news account or, for that matter, between Lord Reith and Lord Haw-Haw, other than what a 'masculine' or 'feminine' or some other discourse happens to make of them.

Finally on 'bias'

The debate on bias in the news has been renewed recently with a series of attacks on broadcasters from Conservative politicians and from right-wing newspapers. From a crude relativist position, we might see these as simply more evidence that the right-wing see the press one way, while the left see it differently, rather as two sets of football supporters might watch the same match but see only the fouls committed by the other side.

However, the debate on bias is too important to be left to the politicians since it is being used by them to justify decisions which are being made about the whole future of broadcasting. I want now to comment on what communications researchers can add to this debate beyond the academic truism that 'bias is not a useful concept since it implies an unbiased true perspective which will be shared by all'. We can accept that there are cultural dimensions to perception and belief, but it does not follow that we should abandon the analysis of news content on criteria such as accuracy, or even balance. We should also be able to comment on the use of such criteria by others, such as political parties, who lay claim to have produced for themselves a 'scientific' analysis of the news.

Let us consider the critique of BBC news coverage produced by Norman Tebbit, in 1986, as chairman of the Conservative Party. This focused on the reporting of the bombing of Libya by American forces in April 1986. The Tebbit report offered practical examples of how the BBC's approach to reporting could be improved. For example, it objected to this introduction to a BBC bulletin:

> We'll be assessing the world reaction to what the Americans have done, and the political repercussions for Mrs. Thatcher.
>
> (BBC, 21.00, 15.4.86)

The report wanted a much more upbeat attitude towards the Americans and suggested the phrase:

> We'll be looking at the events that prompted America's retaliation and its chances of success.
>
> (Conservative Central Office, 1986, p. 8)

The report also wanted the word 'murdered' to be used in describing terrorist actions and objected to the BBC saying that people were 'shot through the head' and 'killed' (p. 22). But as the BBC argues in its reply (1986), the term 'shot through the head' is hardly neutral and in any event the BBC did use the term 'murdered' later on.

Words such as 'killed' and 'dead' are not neutral in their use either. When the Glasgow University Media Group (1985) analysed news coverage of the sinking of the Argentine ship the *Belgrano* during the Falklands war, it was found that journalists avoided the word 'killed' and that nobody was said to have 'died' upon the ship. Words such as 'missing' or 'lost' were frequently used (but the harder terms *were* commonly used for British casualties). It is clear that television news is already partisan in the way that such terms are used. The Tebbit report wanted to take this usage a stage further and to make the news express an open commitment.

A further problem for neutrality in broadcasting is that *many* groups and countries cause people to be killed – but only some are to be called 'terrorist'. When a city is bombed at night, is it an atrocity or merely bad targeting when innocents are killed? Was the photographer who was blown up by French agents on the *Rainbow Warrior* 'murdered' or merely 'lost'? The issue that broadcasters face when they deploy such terms is whether they are reserving the harsher ones simply for perpetrators who are not on 'our' side.

No such worries concerned the authors of the Tebbit report. It is clear on who the enemies and friends are, and how they should be described. The BBC's apparently detached style was a source of irritation. It is not the first time that the BBC has been attacked for lack of commitment. During the Falklands war there were criticisms made of the BBC for referring to 'the British' rather than 'we' or 'us' and the BBC journalist Peter Snow was criticized for using the phrase 'if the British are to be believed'.

At the time, these issues were hotly discussed at the top news and current affairs meetings in the BBC. The minutes of these meetings record one senior broadcaster reminding the meeting that 'the BBC was the *British* Broadcasting Corporation' and stating that 'he believed it was an unnecessary irritation to stick to the detached style' (News and Current Affairs minutes, 11.5.82). The meeting as a whole believed that it was being wrongly accused. Its view is recorded that:

> The weight of BBC coverage had been concerned with government statements and policy. In their vilification of the BBC, the Government seemed to have entirely overlooked this. The meeting endorsed this point.
>
> (NCA, 11.5.82)

This defence, *that they were wrongly accused*, was used again by the BBC in its reply to the Tebbit report. The broadcasters stated that they had given 'the strongest line in favour of Mrs Thatcher's position to appear in any of the headlines, ITN's or the BBC's' (1986, p. 1). The headline to which they refer was:

> Tonight Mrs Thatcher shows her critics the proof of Libyan terrorism.
>
> (BBC1, 21.00, 15.4.86)

They mention this headline on three separate occasions in their reply, describing it as 'a powerful and unqualified statement of fact'. We might note in passing that this 'fact' has been subject to a good deal of questioning. From a very early stage, experts on the Middle East were saying that Syria and Iran were more likely suspects than Libya. A report in the *Observer* carried accusations that the Americans had 'massaged' the evidence (27.4.86). Yet in the face of this the BBC was still happy to state in its reply that it was 'the only organisation to say at the outset that there was proof of such terrorism' (p. 1). As we will see, there is an ambivalence in the broadcaster's response between protecting their right to report facts which politicians find unpleasant, and their defence that they were wrongly accused of doing so.

There was a second strand of criticism in the Tebbit report. It declared whole areas of news to be suspect because they operated 'in Libya's interests'. These areas included criticism of America and coverage of Libyan casualties. According to the Tebbit report, there were just two ways in which the American raid could be interpreted. It was either 'a vicious and illegal attack by a militaristic superpower on a small nation' or it could be seen as 'a legitimate and necessary defensive action'. The first view was attributed by the report to the Libyans and to the British opposition parties (Conservative Central Office, 1986, p. 3). Such an analysis effectively put the SDP, Liberals, Labour, and Libyans all in the same boat. Such a division of viewpoints did in fact misrepresent those people in Britain who criticized the American action while remaining severely critical of Colonel Gaddafi and his regime. It would also be wrong to assume that, because television featured criticisms of America, this in any way implied support for the Libyan leader. Indeed, if the Tebbit report had looked beyond the two BBC programmes which it chose, it could have found news coverage which was positively rude about Gaddafi. For example, in a later programme, a *Newsnight* reporter commented that:

> The homespun philosophy of his little green books looks more and more threadbare, out of touch, even as he struts Libya's tiny stage dreaming his fanciful dream.
>
> (BBC2, 29.7.86))

The Tebbit report was also concerned that coverage of the effects of the bombing was in Libya's interests. It accepted that the casualties would be covered, but objected to them being given prominence in the news. It has this to say of the BBC coverage:

> The BBC then chose a particularly damaging phrase to describe America's response, '*in Washington the mood is one of jubilation*', which, when sandwiched between phrases such as '*children are casualties*' and '*causing deaths and injuries to men, women and children as they slept in their homes*', suggested extreme callousness.
>
> It also devoted far more of the opening paragraph than ITN did to words and phrases designed to arouse anti-American emotion: 'across the world there is great concern'.
>
> '*Deaths and injuries to men, women and children as they slept in their homes*', '*Colonel Gaddafi's own family was hit*', '*in intensive care with serious injuries*'.
>
> The point is not whether these statements should be made but whether they should be given such prominence in the first, 'audience conditioning' part of the report.
>
> (Conservative Central Office, 1986, p. 7; italics in original)

The Tebbit report also argued that coverage of civilian deaths and injuries should be accompanied by a warning that it is 'Libyan-controlled' (in the sense that journalists were allowed to film civilian but not military areas). In passing, we might try to think how many countries would take foreign journalists on a tour of their military installations five hours after they had been bombed. However, the BBC's reply is that they did indeed make more than seventy references to reporting restrictions in their coverage as a whole.

The strongest parts of the BBC's defence are when they stop claiming that they were wrongly accused and instead refute one of the basic premises of the Tebbit report – that they should be concerned with how damaging their news coverage is and whose interests are served by it:

> It is not the BBC's function to decide whether some facts are too 'damaging' or too 'callous' to be broadcast; and if we were to take that decision we would indeed be open to the accusation of manipulating the news for political purposes.
>
> (BBC Response, November 1986, p. 6)[25]

ITN received special praise from Mr Tebbit for stating clearly that 'the Libyans are now trying to use the American's raid as a propaganda weapon for themselves' (ITN, 22.00, 15.4.86). We seem to be back on the terrain of making distinctions between two types of victims – 'ours' who are simply innocent and 'theirs' who are propaganda. If television coverage rejects such a distinction and chooses to highlight the fate of innocent casualties, then it is applying an even-handed criterion to news reporting. It is asserting the basic right to be innocent, whichever country the casualties happen to be in. By contrast, the Tebbit Report wanted to substitute a system of two types of reporting – one for 'us' and one for 'them'. If the right to be innocent is downgraded in this way, then it does make sense to have the upbeat introduction which the Conservatives desired and to reduce the prominence of statements about casualties. But it is an extraordinary demand to make of a news organization such as the BBC which sees itself as being concerned with fairness, balance, and the expression of basic human and democratic values.

The prime concern of the Conservative critique of the BBC was whose *interests* would be served by what was reported. This constitutes a major change in the standards which are to be applied to broadcasting. It is not two sets of supporters seeing the match differently, but is equivalent to moving the goal-posts.

One important task for communication researchers is to identify such changes in the currents of political debate. We should not be content to write off political attacks on television as being no more than the differently situated perceptions of subgroups.

We might ask, would the politicians themselves accept the view that the reception of news depends simply upon political predispositions? If they did believe this, then there would be few grounds for complaint as the same news account would be 'read' one way by Conservatives and a different way by Labour supporters. They do not accept such a view exactly because they understand that some images, such as children being taken from the rubble of bombs, cannot easily be justified within any current audience perspective.

One of the key findings of my own study is that our political views are not inviolate or 'sealed off' in a private conceptual space. Our beliefs are often subject to being challenged and reworked in relation to new information. The images of violence in the miners' strike did concern and depress some who were otherwise very sympathetic to the miners' cause. At the same time, others in the audience who were not especially sympathetic were able to criticize the television images by deploying arguments on the inaccuracy, selectivity, and contradiction within news accounts. This indicates that it is possible to produce a rational critique of media content whose validity can be argued for beyond the preferences of a given political subculture. A further task for communication researchers is to produce such critiques and to inform the public debate both on the nature of news accounts and the validity of the political criticisms which are made of them. We should not abandon this task. If we do so, we abandon our own ability to criticize and to comment on the validity, consistency, and accuracy of the arguments which are deployed. Meanwhile, the real power struggles over broadcasting will continue as the cultural theorists marginalize themselves and drift off into the mists of relativism. It is clear that questions about the influence of the press and television on popular belief should be high on the agenda of communications research. This book does point to the powerful impact of the media, both in limiting what audiences can see and in providing key elements of political consciousness and belief.

Appendix 1

Types of 'news' produced by the groups

General sample

Croydon solicitors	– Trade union news, 2 BBC news
Glasgow solicitors	– Channel 4/Alternative trade union news, 3 BBC news
LT catering staff	– 3 BBC news
LT catering supervisors	– Trade union news, BBC news
Electronics staff	– 3 BBC news
Glasgow retirement group	– Trade union news, 2 BBC news, Conservative news/editorial
Glasgow women	– Trade union/Channel 4 news, 2 BBC news
Bromley women	– Trade union news, BBC news
Penge women	– 2 news programmes
Bromley residents	– Trade union news, BBC news
Beckenham residents	– Trade union news, 3 BBC news
Shenfield residents	– Trade union news, BBC news, ITN news

Groups with special knowledge/experience

Police	– Trade union news, police news, 2 BBC news
Scottish trade unionists	– 3 Trade union news, 2 BBC news
Yorkshire miners/women's support group	– Trade union news, BBC news
Print workers	– Trade union news, BBC news

Appendix 2

Tables of results from questions 1, 4, 6, 7, and 8

The results from questions 2, 3, 9, and 10 are not tabulated here as they were not intended to provide original research data, but were used as a backup to other questions. Question 5 is also not tabulated as the replies to it were almost unanimous.

Question 1: Who did the gun belong to?

Question 4: Was picketing violent or mostly peaceful?

Question 6: Reasons given for rejecting the view that picketing was mostly violent

Question 7: 'On news most'

Question 8: 'Most personal impact'

Question 1: Who did the gun belong to?

General Sample	Miners shooting rabbits/poacher/farmer	Striking miner/picket	National Front	Media plant	Miners' family	Police plant	Police weapon	Non-police source	Need more information to comment	Not associate with strike	Outsider/infiltrator/troublemaker/militant/activist/agitator	Working miner
Croydon solicitors		7			1						1	
Glasgow solicitors		13	1				1				2	1
LT catering staff						1	4				2	
LT catering supervisors		3								2	1	
Electronics staff	1	6					2				2	
Glasgow retirement group		5					2			1	6	
Glasgow women		5				2				1	2	
Bromley women		7								2		
Penge women		6					2				1	
Bromley residents		4					2			2	1	
Beckenham residents		8					1			3		
Shenfield residents		5					1			1	2	1
TOTALS	1	69	1		1	3	15			12	20	2

Groups with special knowledge/experience												
Police		5						1	2			
Scottish trade unionists	1	3		1		7	1			4	1	1
Yorkshire miners/WSG	2					7						
Print workers		3				2					4	
TOTALS	3	11		1		16	1	1	2	4	5	1

Question 4: Was picketing mostly violent or mostly peaceful?

General Sample	Mostly violent	Mostly peaceful	Unsure
Croydon solicitors	4	5	
Glasgow solicitors	3	14	1
LT catering staff	7		
LT catering supervisors	3	3	
Electronics staff	7	4	
Glasgow retirement group	10	3	1
Glasgow women	6	4	
Bromley women	5	3	1
Penge women	4	4	
Bromley residents	4	5	
Beckenham residents	10	2	
Shenfield residents	3	6	1
TOTALS	66	53	4

Groups with special knowledge/experience			
Police		8	
Scottish trade unionists	3	16	
Yorkshire miners/WSG		9	
Print workers	1	8	
TOTALS	4	41	

Question 6: Reasons given for rejecting the view that picketing was mostly violent

General sample	At or near picket lines/knew miners or police	Union information	Deduction based on amount of picketing	TV/press select and exaggerate	Experience of TV/press reporting	Comparison of different media accounts	Belief that most people peaceful	Violence shown to discredit miners
Croydon solicitors	2			4	1	3		
Glasgow solicitors	4		3	4	1	7	1	
LT catering staff								
LT catering supervisors	1			1				1
Electronics staff	2	1	2	1			1	
Glasgow retirement group	2			1				
Bromley women				1		3		
Penge women			1	1		1	1	
Bromley residents	3		1	1		1		
Beckenham residents	1			1				
Shenfield residents	3			1		3		
TOTALS	18	1	7	16	2	18	3	1

Groups with special knowledge/experience								
Police	8							
Scottish trade unionists	11	2	2	1				
Yorkshire miners/WSG	9							
Print workers	3		1	4	2			
TOTALS	31	2	3	5	2			

Question 7: 'On news most'

General sample	Confrontation/clashes/ picketing/violence	Victimizing/attacks on working miners	Violence on police	Taxi-driver/concrete block killing	Police presence	Return to work	Nottinghamshire miners working	Numbers on strike	Lorries moving coal
Croydon solicitors	7	1							
Glasgow solicitors	15								
LT catering staff	7								
LT catering supervisors	6								
Electronics staff	7								
Glasgow retirement group	8				2				
Bromley women	8	2	1		1				
Penge women	8	1				1			
Bromley residents	6								
Beckenham residents	6								
Shenfield residents	3								
TOTALS	81	4	1		3	1			

Groups with special knowledge/experience									
Police	3							1	
Scottish trade unionists	17			1		4			
Yorkshire miners/WSG	5					5			1
Print workers						6	2		
TOTALS	25			1		15	2	1	1

General Sample	Mining communities/ miners lives	Hardship	Miners in the wrong	Negotiations/meetings arguments, Scargill/ MacGregor/Government	Arthur Scargill	Ian MacGregor	NCB	Conservative Ministers	Militants
Croydon solicitors				1	2				
Glasgow solicitors				2	2	1			
LT catering staff					1				
LT catering supervisors	1	1							
Electronics staff				3	6	2	1		
Glasgow retirement group			1		4				2
Bromley women				1	3	1			
Penge women				1					
Bromley residents		3		1					
Beckenham residents					6				
Shenfield residents				1	6				
TOTALS	1	4	1	10	30	4	1		2

Groups with special knowledge/experience									
Police				3	1				
Scottish trade unionists			1	1	2		1		
Yorkshire miners/WSG					1	1		1	
Print workers				1		1			
TOTALS			1	5	4	2	1	1	

Question 8: 'Most personal impact'

General sample	Confrontation/ clashes/picketing violence	Violence to police	Police violence/police charging miners/police causing trouble	Police presence/in riot gear	Intimidation (victimization) of working miners/ strikebreakers	Taxi-driver/concrete block killing	Woman, brick through car window	Orgreave	Union troublemaking	Coaches and cars being stopped on motorway
Croydon solicitors	2		1			1			1	
Glasgow solicitors	1	1	3	1	3	3	1			
LT catering staff	3		2							
LT catering supervisors	3					2				
Electronics staff	3					2				
Glasgow retirement group	4	1	4							
Bromley women	6		1			1				
Penge women	2									
Bromley residents		1				1				
Beckenham residents	4	2	1		3					
Shenfield residents	2		2		1					
TOTALS	30	5	14	1	7	10	1		1	

Groups with special knowledge/experience										
Police			3			1				
Scottish trade unionists	4		4	1	1	2				
Yorkshire miners/WSG			3					2		
Print workers			3				1			1
TOTALS	4		13	1	1	3	1	2		1

General sample	Bitterness/divided families/communities	Return to work	Lorries moving coal	Hardship/loss of money/ jobs/closing mines	Waste of time, effort/ length/cost	Breakdown of union solidarity	Breakaway of UDM	Strength of mining communities	Miners' wives in strike	Arthur Scargill
Croydon solicitors	2				3					3
Glasgow solicitors	1	1		1						3
LT catering staff	2	1		2						
LT catering supervisors	4									1
Electronics staff				1						3
Glasgow retirement				2			1		1	2
Bromley women							1			2
Penge women	1			2	2					3
Bromley residents	3				2					3
Beckenham residents	1			1					1	1
Shenfield residents	3			1	1			1		3
TOTALS	17	2		10	8		2	1	2	24

Groups with special knowledge/experience										
Police	2			1						
Scottish trade unionists		1		2				1	3	2
Yorkshire miners/WSG		2								
Print workers			2			2				
TOTALS	2	3	2	3		2		1	3	2

General sample

	Ian MacGregor	Mick McGahey	Margaret Thatcher	Hard-line attitude of Government/NCB	Obstinacy/ intransigence	Inadequate leadership of miners	Effects of cameras on pickets	Biased media coverage	Amount of media coverage
Croydon solicitors									1
Glasgow solicitors			1	1					
LT catering staff									
LT catering supervisors									
Electronics staff	1				1				
Glasgow retirement group		1		1	1				
Bromley women									
Penge women									
Bromley residents	1								
Beckenham residents									
Shenfield residents	2				1	2	1		
TOTALS	4	1	1	2	3	2	1		1

Groups with special knowledge/experience									
Police									
Scottish trade unionists				2				5	
Yorkshire miners/WSG								2	
Print workers									
TOTALS				2				7	

Notes

Introduction

1 See, for example, Jane Root's (1986) commentary on the problems of laboratory-based experiments on children's reactions to screen violence: '. . . these experiments are actually highly suspect, not least because of the difficulty of mimicking people's reactions in a laboratory. Experimental situations always create their own keenness to please the interviewer. . . .' (p. 14).

2 Katz and Lazarsfeld (1955) studied the influence of small groups on the communication process, suggesting that messages were first interpreted and then relayed by 'opinion leaders'. This, they claimed, acted as a block on media influence because the primary group formed a protective screen around the individual. But as Bramson (1961) notes, it is not clear why in principle the opinion leaders could not be influenced by media messages and thus relay a specific view to their 'group'.

   My own study shows that some messages were apparently being absorbed from the media without discussion or reference to peers. The group meetings which were held for this study sometimes acted as a catalyst for beliefs to be discussed, and then changes did occur in relation to 'peer' opinions which were expressed.

3 See, for example, the account in Cassata and Asante (1979). In Britain the uses and gratifications perspective was associated with theorists such as Trenaman and McQuail (1961). They examined the effects on voters of exposure to election broadcasts and political views. Their research suggested that there was no significant relation between exposure and change of opinion. Later studies found more 'effect' upon less committed voters (Blumler and McQuail, 1968).

4 This conclusion has also been challenged by Charles Wright (1986) who argues that the findings of the early theorists such as Lazarsfeld were misinterpreted by later scholars. Wright notes that: 'I have yet to find the conclusion in Lazarsfeld's research that mass communication (or the mass media) is either socially or sociologically unimportant. Nor does the research show that mass communication has "no effect" ' (1986, p. 29).

5 Thus early work by theorists such as J. Blumler (1964) studied how

the development of attitudes to political parties related simply to the 'amount of exposure to television politics' (p. 230).

6 See, for example, the analysis of political news by the Glasgow University Media Group (1982).

7 See, for example, Hartmann and Husband (1972) on the coverage of 'race' in the media and the Glasgow University Media Group (1976 and 1980) on television coverage of industrial and economic issues. There has also been work on how the news 'agenda' can vary in relation to prevailing political forces. See, for example, the Glasgow University Media Group (1985) study of television reporting on the Falklands War.

8 Thus Graham Murdock and David Morley have argued that we must move away from the focus on individual needs and interests which characterizes the uses and gratifications approach. They examine how individual differences may be culturally based and located within frameworks of meaning which vary between subcultures within the audience (Murdock, 1973; Morley, 1980).

1 Making the news

1 For examples of the pictures see pp. 13–18.

2 There were also two further pilots conducted with a group of ten residents from St Albans, Herts., and ten women from community/nursery groups in Glasgow (see Chapter 4).

3 A list of the types of 'news' produced by the various groups is given in Appendix 1.

4 In the early stages of the research, questions 4 and 5 were asked in different ways, shifting the emphasis between peace and violence to see if it made any difference. Thus one group was asked whether TV images of picketing were 'mostly violent' and a different group whether they were 'mostly peaceful'. It apparently made no difference as everyone in both groups saw the TV images as overwhelmingly violent. They seemed to have very clear views on this, and the questions were then asked as above.

5 The importance of looking at group processes is shown in work by Franka Odeka at Glasgow University. She has examined the effectiveness of 'enlightenment campaigns' in the third world. Her method includes making videos of the responses of groups of children who were watching government-sponsored advertising. The advertisements consisted of exhortations on issues such as staying in Nigeria rather than emigrating. In one of these a character, 'Andrew' is shown leaving the country, but at the last moment a stern hand is placed on his shoulder and he is told that he should stay. In the video Andrew is presented as a super-cool stylish figure, very much

the 'bad guy' at the end of the street. However, some of the children watching clearly identify with him. In one group, children can be seen emulating his walk and mannerisms as they play while watching the video. This is the opposite of what the programme-makers intended and might be a difficult research finding to elicit using a face-to-face interview technique. But the group shots show it quite clearly (Franka Odeka, fieldwork for Ph.D thesis, University of Glasgow, 1988).

2 Practical experience and knowledge

1 ITN was thought to be 'the same', but six people made the exception of Channel 4 news, saying that it gave a fairer view.
2 They were happier about the quality press, which they all said they preferred to read.
3 Views of ITN were more mixed and the group was divided between seeing it as 'right-wing', 'left-wing', 'middle-of-the-road' and 'sensationalist'. This mixture of attitudes was common in the groups as a whole and relates in part to the advent of Channel 4 news, which was often seen as more 'alternative' in its approach.

3 Occupational groups

1 This exchange is interesting since it shows how the perception of an image can be affected by belief. But the image cannot indefinitely be re-defined in this way as at some stage the meaning has to be justified to other members of the group. This was done here by reference to the 'actual' content of the picture.

4 Special interest groups

1 In the early stages of the exercise, it had also been commented by one person that the BBC might have been 'left-wing' because of the frequent appearances of Arthur Scargill, but this did not appear in the written answers.
2 We must also bear in mind that the same word, such as 'militant', may be used by people who have a different analysis of the situation, and the word may thus have a variety of connotations. It could be part of a right-wing perspective which saw working-class people as gullible and 'easily led' by trouble-makers/militants. It could be used, as we have seen, by people who do not believe miners as a body are violent, and therefore choose an outside/minority group to blame. Or, someone who is actually a militant might see the word as connoting simply 'the authentic leadership of the work-

ing class'. This does show how we must understand the meaning of words used in the context of the explanations within which they are generated.

3 On this basis two older women also attended the first group.

5 Residential groups

1 I did not comment on the gun or on 'picket violence', which occurred as a phrase in their story. In the event both stories were interesting for the number of references to events which did not relate to the pictures.

6 Conclusions: news content and audience belief

1 This was ironic since she was in fact not the only one in this group with such sympathies. Two others had also had the experience of moving from the north to the south.

2 See, for example, Colin Sweet, 'Why coal is under attack – nuclear powers in the energy establishment', in Beynon (1985). It was also argued that the government's desire to defeat the miners after the successful strikes of 1972 and 1974 was a major reason in its own right for their interest in nuclear power. The miners themselves had developed their own arguments on nuclear power and privatization in the series of campaign booklets published shortly before the strike. See Nicholas Jones (1986), p. 175.

3 Martin Adeney and John Lloyd also point to the extensive links between the media and some government members, notably Peter Walker (Adeney and Lloyd, 1986, pp. 244–5).

4 Thus Martin Adeney and John Lloyd write that before the strike started 'the option of continuing to cut capacity without necessarily triggering industrial action did appear available' (1986, p. 70).

5 Estimates for the total cost of the dispute varied, but were always expressed in 'billions' of pounds. The additional electricity costs alone were put at £2,000 million (ITN, 13.2.85). None of this included the economic costs of redundancy and unemployment, also paid by the state, as pits were closed. In this sample there was only one mention of such costs, by one person in the Glasgow retirement group.

6 These percentages are based on the number of people who answered each question. The number varies because the Glasgow women's group was included for some questions and in the Penge group one woman had to leave before completing her answers.

7 None of these elements are static and they can all move in relation to each other. For example, several people said that their beliefs

about television had been altered by what they had seen. They had believed it to be neutral until its presentation of the miners strike. This potential for change is important since there is a recent trend in media studies to present the interpretation of television messages as being subject to pre-existing cultural and political beliefs. Such beliefs are important dimensions to the reception of new information, but they cannot be treated as fixed entities. There is the constant possibility of their movement and renegotiation in relation to what we see and are told and as a result of new experience.

7 Issues in news content, effects, and 'bias'

1 After the strike had ended a BBC *Brass Tacks* programme gave a further account of events at Orgreave. They used a video shot by the police at the time and invited an ex-chief constable, John Alderson, to comment on what it showed about the escalation of violence. He concludes that 'although there was pushing and shoving by the miners and one or two throwing missiles of one kind or another . . . the first escalation, it seems to me, came from the cantering of the horses into the crowd which merely heightened the tension and increased the violence – which is contrary to what the police stand for. The police are there to diminish violence not increase it' (*Brass Tacks*, 31.10.85). This extract was later used in a programme made by GUMG with the BBC. It compared the initial BBC news on Orgreave with the *Brass Tacks* programme ('Bias in the News', 10.3.86).
2 There were reports at the time that the initial impetus to publish the figures had come from the government. The *Observer* reported that 'It was at the Prime Minister's urging that the NCB began to publish back-to-work figures' (25.11.84).
3 See, for example, Philo, Beharrell, and Hewitt (1977).
4 They in fact make the same comparison used earlier by the GUMG in 'Bias in the News' (BBC2, 10.3.86) (see above, note 1).
5 Colin Sparks also criticizes this conclusion in his review of the study. See Sparks (1987) and the rejoinders from David Morrison (1987) and John Brown *et al.* (1987).
6 There have been many attempts to analyse news content by focusing on the use of individual words. For example, Paul Hartmann (1975/6) examined industrial news coverage and drew up a list of relevant adjectives. He kept a record of the number of occasions that any of these were applied to the main categories of participant. The second most frequent adjective applied to workers in his material was that of 'militant'. But we need to know the context in which such a word appears. It is possible for it to be applied to a sector of the workforce in a sense of 'endangering the community

through fanatical actions'. Equally it could be used in the context of a group of workers who in their own view are setting a positive example of the type of action which the rest of the workforce should follow. There is no necessary meaning which can be attributed to single words which are abstracted from their context in the news. A similar point is made above in relation to the use of the word 'militant' by audience groups.

7 Such approaches are often characterized as 'positivist' in that they neglect actors' meanings and the processes by which they are generated. The origin of such methods is in what their proponents see as the methods of the natural sciences. Human relations are treated as fixed, measurable pieces of data. As Phillipson and Roche comment, the problem is 'the nature of the fit between abstract sociological concepts, which turn out to be convenient shorthand for subsuming "large masses of unintelligible data" and the interaction sequences to which they purport to refer. In the event the fit is managed by fiat; correspondence is forced or is merely assumed' (Phillipson and Roche, 1971).

8 A corollary of this is that social relations also underpin the generation of descriptions by social scientists. It might be argued that language, perception and the development of theory itself is conditioned by social structure. All social analysis presupposes assumptions on the nature of what is to be measured. These assumptions inform the selection of data, the formation of analytic categories and the causal relationships which can be posited. Reality is not, therefore, something which is simply 'out there' waiting to be measured – a neutral set of 'facts'. Rather, what can be seen in the reality depends in part upon assumptions that are held of what the reality is, and of what are the relations which produce it as it is. The importance of this is that there can, therefore, be no general method which simply assembles 'all' the data to be used by all the approaches. For the assumptions on the nature of what is being examined affect the direction and the organization of the investigation. The description that the social scientist offers is also affected by his view of what is 'important' to his own investigation and of its significance to his audience. In a critique of our work, Anderson and Sharrock comment that it would not be possible to reconstruct a whole news programme from the accounts which we have given. But as phenomenologists, they will know that no descriptions are ever exhaustive, but are always curtailed on criteria of relevance and significance. Thus if there is a general belief that the news should interview both 'sides' in a dispute and our research shows that this did not happen, then our audience might see this as significant and 'unfair'. They might see it as more significant in terms of their own beliefs

in this area than, for example, the colour of the newscaster's tie, which has been omitted in the description of the programmes. See Anderson and Sharrock (1979) and the reply by Graham Murdock (1980).

9 It was also our view that such a 'thematic' analysis was a useful corrective to free floating speculation in some research as to the 'meaning' of specific texts. Thus John Corner and Sylvia Harvey have commented on 'the need for complementary and detailed economic, institutional and audience related research if "cultural readings" are not to float free, born aloft on exhilaratingly speculative breezes, from the specific political, economic and social circumstances within which media texts are produced, distributed and interpreted' (1979). This was written in a critique of John Fiske and John Hartley's *Reading Television* (1978), which does indeed drift towards speculation about how certain images might be understood.

10 Having said this it is clear that a decision to focus on strikes as 'industrial news' rather than, for example, management mistakes or investment failures, etc., is itself a value judgement. The reporting of apparently basic information such as which unions are involved clearly begins from such judgements on the relative importance of strikes as industrial stories.

11 This perspective in the analysis of mass communications had been developed in Britain in the work of Stuart Hall and Graham Murdock. Their main concern was to understand what they saw as the ideological discourse of a class society and to show how news talk was underpinned by consensual values. See, for example, Stuart Hall, 'A World at One with Itself' (1970) and Graham Murdock, 'Political Deviance – the Press Presentation of a Militant Mass Demonstration' (1981). Stuart Hall later went on to produce theoretical commentaries on the relation between the 'encoding' of messages within specific frameworks of meaning and their 'decoding' by those who received them in the audience (1980).

12 Some critics misunderstood this dimension of our method. Anderson and Sharrock (1979) thought that we were giving a special credence to some sources such as the *Financial Times* – as if we were saying that their account was 'true' as compared with that of the news. But our interest was in looking at the range of explanations which were available.

We also examined the 'common ground' which existed on some issues such as whether wages were the source of inflationary pressure. We noted for example that the *Economist* had accepted that it was Britain's failure on productivity rather than wages which made it inflation-prone. Alistair Burnett (1980) of ITN took exception to this, commenting that the *Economist* at that time had taken a rather conservative view on the need for statutory wage control. But such differences in political strategy should not pre-empt the possibility of there being some mutually agreed information.

13 Stuart Hall discusses this in terms of a 'structure in dominance', which is sustained through actively winning the consent of subordinate classes and groups. See his discussion of the work of Althusser and Gramsci in relation to this (1977). For evidence of the broadcaster's desire to defend their own formal independence, see the controversy over reporting during the Falklands war, as discussed by Robert Harris (1983) and the Glasgow University Media Group (1985).

14 But even in this area there have been controversies which indicate that some journalists are prepared to contest the limits of 'acceptable reporting'. Some critics have suggested that the content of television news merely reflects the prevailing balance of forces in the society. But just as this 'balance' is constantly contested, so the manner in which competing views are reproduced is also the site of struggle. If the parameters of acceptable journalism were not constantly subject to being re-drawn (by politicians as well as by journalists), there would be no controversy over television coverage. See Ian Connell's critique of the Glasgow studies (1980) and the replies by Philo, Hewitt and Beharrell (1980).

15 Doris Graber (1984) in a study of American audience groups shows how people extract limited amounts of information from news stories, which they consider important for their thinking. She terms this the schema process which 'does well in reducing the danger of information overload [but] does not lead to the retention of a large amount of factual data. Understanding rather than rote learning, is the goal' (p. 202).

16 Their results here are not altogether consistent. If we follow their train of thought, we might expect more Conservative voters than Labour to believe that the cameras are located behind the pickets. But in fact their results show exactly the opposite, with double the percentage of Labour voters believing this (12 per cent) as against Conservatives (6 per cent).

17 As defined in Althusser's *For Marx* (1969), the problematic is 'the theoretical or ideological framework in which [a concept] is used. . . . It is centred on the absence of problems and concepts . . . as much as their presence' (p. 252). Althusser posits a system of interrelated structures which determine various levels of the social formation – the theoretical, economic, political, etc. His perspective has been criticized for its limited view of social action and consciousness. See, for example, E.P. Thompson's *The Poverty of Theory* (1978).

18 There may also be periods in social development where a dominant

class has been relatively successful in sustaining the consent of key sections of the population and a degree of consensus prevails, such that the dominant belief systems may be established as the 'common sense' of a high proportion of those in the society. The relation between such common sense and 'alternative' philosophies is thus likely to vary with specific social and historical conditions. In the period of this research there were apparently very sharp divisions of political opinion which perhaps indicated the break-up of some elements of the traditional consensus associated with post-war Britain. A more extended analysis of the implications of consensual assumptions in news reporting is given in David Morley's (1981) study of the content of industrial news.

19 A third reason why we do not inhabit discrete problematics which determine our perception of the 'real' is provided by E.P. Thompson (1978) in his powerful critique of Althusserian philosophy. He argues that we share specific experiences of real objects in the world and that the 'objective' world imposes limits on what can be achieved. In making a table, for example, the nature of the wood determines what *cannot* be done with it:

> I see my table. To be an object, to be 'null and inert', does not remove that object from being a determining party within a subject-object relation. No piece of timber has ever been known to make itself into a table: no joiner has ever been known to make a table out of air, or sawdust. The joiner appropriates that timber and, in working it up into a table, he is governed both by his skills (theoretical practice, itself arising from a history, or 'experience', of making tables, as well as a history of the evolution of appropriate tools) and by the qualities (size, grain, seasoning etc.) of the timber . . . the wood cannot determine what is made, nor whether it is made well or badly, but it can certainly determine what cannot be made, the limits (size, strength etc.) of what is made, and the skills and tools appropriate to the determined properties of its real object, and must operate within this determined field. If it breaks free, then it becomes engaged in freakish speculative botching, and the self-extrapolation of a 'knowledge' of tables out of pre-existent bigotry. Since this 'knowledge' does not correspond to the reality of the wood, it will very soon demonstrate its own 'adequacy or inadequacy' as soon as we sit down at it, it is likely to collapse, spilling its whole load of elaborate epistimological sauces to the floor.
>
> (1978, pp. 17–18)

20 Fiske's analysis is within the post-structuralist tradition and draws extensively on the work of theorists such as Roland Barthes. He uses

Barthes' division between 'readerly and writerly' texts and compares it with Umberto Eco's (1979) categorization of them as 'closed' and 'open'. Both Morley and Fiske owe something to Eco's (1972) work on 'aberrant decoding' – the theory that social differences between the encoder and the decoder will produce alternative 'readings' of the message.

21 There is also a problem with Fiske's conclusions on what male and female preferences actually are. It seems likely that some preferences in news programming relate more to the content of what is shown than to its structure. Morley, in fact, indicates that women *are* interested in certain types of news. He writes that the pattern of preferences 'varies when we consider local news programmes, which a number of the women claim to like. In several cases they give very cogent reasons for this – as they don't understand what the "pound going up or down" is about, and as it has no experiential bearing on their lives they're not interested in it. However, if there has been a crime (for instance, a rape) in their local area, they feel they need to know about it, both for their own sake and their children's sakes' (1986, p. 169). Such a preference apparently relates to content and is not because the news has abandoned its formal claims to objectivity in favour of a 'feminine format'.

22 In December 1988, the *Sun* agreed to pay Elton John £1 million damages to conclude a libel action relating to this story and others printed about him.

23 These trends in German public opinion were reflected in a later poll, which was reported as finding that 'far more West Germans have a positive attitude to current Soviet foreign policy than to President Reagan's. Among better-educated West Germans, the trend is even more pronounced, with 70 per cent judging Soviet policies favourably and 52 per cent having a negative attitude to American ones. Even among Dr Kohl's CDU and CSU supporters, support for Mr Gorbachev's foreign policy is higher than for Mr Reagan's' (*Guardian*, 19.10.88).

24 For an extended discussion of this see Thomas Kuhn, *The Structure of Scientific Revolutions* (1962). His argument is that the development of new paradigms in the natural sciences does not follow simply from the discovery of new evidence, but is affected by social factors such as the growth of professional scientific groups.

25 More surprisingly, the BBC also stated that they had filmed scenes 'which would have suited Gaddafi's propaganda purpose extremely well' (BBC Response, 1986, p. 15). But these scenes, which included 'lines of bodies' and 'relatives screaming and weeping', were deliberately not shown. We might agree that some pictures should be barred because they were horrific, but why not transmit the shots

of the relatives? This *did* seem to have been a clear decision to limit the emotional impact. Here again the BBC is ambivalent between saying that it is wrongly accused and defending its right to report what politicians find unpleasant. This might indeed reflect compromises being made within the organization which have been pointed to elsewhere. See for example 'The Taming of the BBC', *World in Action* (ITV, 29.2.88).

Bibliography

Adeney, M., and Lloyd, J. (1986) *The Miners' Strike*, London, Routledge and Kegan Paul.

Adorno, T., *et al.* (1950) *The Authoritarian Personality*, New York, Harper & Row.

Althusser, L. (1969) *For Marx*, London, Penguin.

Althusser, L. (1971) 'Ideology and Ideological State Apparatuses', in *Lenin and Philosophy*, London, New Left Books.

Anderson, D., and Sharrock, W. (1979) ' "Biasing the News": Technical Issues in "Media Studies" ', *Sociology*, Vol. 13, No. 3.

Barker, M. (1988) 'News Bias and the Miners' Strike', *Media, Culture and Society*, Vol. 10, No. 1.

Barthes, R. (1973) *Mythologies*, London, Paladin.

Barthes, R. (1975) *S/Z*, London, Cape.

BBC (1986) Response to Conservative Central Office Media Monitoring, November 1986.

Berry, C. (1986) 'Message Misunderstood', *Listener*, 27 November 1986.

Berry, C., and Clifford, B. (1986) *Learning from Television News*, IBA/NELP report.

Beynon, H. (ed.) (1985) *Digging Deeper*, London, Verso.

Blumler, J. (1964) 'British Television – a Research Strategy', *British Journal of Sociology*, Vol. 15, No. 3.

Blumler, J., and McQuail, D. (1968) *Television in Politics: Its Uses and Influence*, London, Faber and Faber.

Bramson, L. (1961) *The Political Context of Sociology*, Princeton, Princeton University Press.

Brown, J., McGregor, R., and Cumberbatch, G. (1987) 'Tilting at Windmills', *Media, Culture and Society*, Vol. 9, No. 4.

Brunsdon, C., and Morley, D. (1978) *Everyday Television: Nationwide*, London, BFI.

Burnett, A. (1980) Speech to the Royal Television Society, 29 May 1980.

Burnie, J. (1986) 'The Things We Do', *Daily Record*, 23 May 1986.
Cantril, H., *et al.* (1940) *The Invasion From Mars: A Study in the Psychology of Panic*, Princeton, Princeton University Press.
Cassata, M., and Asante, M. (1979) *Mass Communication*, New York, Macmillan.
Central Office of Information/HMSO (1988) AIDS, Monitoring Response to the Public Education Campaign, February 1986–February 1987, ISBN 011321096/5.
Cockerell, M., Hennessy, P., and Walker, D. (1984) *Sources Close to the Prime Minister*, London, Macmillan.
Collett, P., and Lamb, R. (1985) *Watching People Watching Television*, IBA report.
Connell, I. (1978) 'The Reception of Television Science', Primary Communications Research Centre, University of Leicester.
Connell, I. (1980) Review of *More Bad News, Marxism Today*, August.
Conservative Central Office (1986) Media Monitoring Report, October 1986.
Corner, J., and Harvey, S. (1979) 'The Cultural Reading of Television', *Communication Studies Bulletin*, No. 5.
Crick, M. (1985) 'Reporting the Strike', *Granta*, 15.
Cumberbatch, G. (1986) 'Bias that lies in the Eye of the Beholder', *Guardian*, 19 May 1986.
Cumberbatch, G., McGregor, R., Brown, J., and Morrison, D. (1986) *Television and the Miners' Strike*, London, BFI Broadcasting Research Unit.
Cumberbatch, G., Brown, J., McGregor, R., and Morrison, D. (1988) 'Arresting Knowledge', *Media, Culture and Society*, Vol. 10, No. 1.
Curtis, L. (1984) *Ireland: the Propaganda War*, London, Pluto.
Davis, H., and Walton, P. (eds) (1983) *Language, Image, Media*, London, Blackwell.
Eco, U. (1972) 'Towards a Semiotic Inquiry into the TV Message', in Corner, J., and Hawthorn, J. (eds) (1980) *Communication Studies: an Introductory Reader*, London, Edward Arnold.
Eco, U. (1979) *The Role of the Reader: Explorations in the Semiotics of Texts*, Bloomington and London, Indiana University Press.
Eldridge, J. (1987) 'Mass Media, Public Opinion and Democ-

racy', Presidential address at Belfast, British Association for the Advancement of Science.
Findahl, O., and Höijer, B. (1985) 'Some Characteristics of News Memory and Comprehension', *Journal of Electronic and Broadcasting Media*, Vol. 29, No. 4.
Fiske, J. (1987a) *Television Culture*, London, Methuen.
Fiske, J. (1987b) 'British Cultural Studies and Television', in Allen, R. (ed.) *Channels of Discourse*, London, Methuen.
Fiske, J., and Hartley, J. (1978) *Reading Television*, London, Methuen.
Frank, R.S. (1973) *Message Dimensions of Television News*, Massachusetts, Lexington Books, D.C. Heath.
Gerbner, G., *et al.* (1977) 'Television Violence Profile No. 8: The Highlights', *Journal of Communication*, Vol. 27.
Gerbner, G., *et al.* (1978) 'Cultural Indicators: Violence Profile No. 8', *Journal of Communications*, Vol. 28.
Gerbner, G., *et al.* (1979) 'The Demonstration of Power: Violence Profile No. 10', *Journal of Communication*, Vol. 29.
Gerbner, G., *et al.* (1986) 'Living With Television: The Dynamics of the Cultivation Process', in Bryant, J., and Zillmann, D. (eds) *Perspectives on Media Effects*, Hillsdale, New Jersey, and London, Lawrence Erlbaum Associates.
Glasgow University Media Group (1976) *Bad News*, London, Routledge and Kegan Paul.
Glasgow University Media Group (1980) *More Bad News*, London, Routledge and Kegan Paul.
Glasgow University Media Group (1982) *Really Bad News*, London, Writers and Readers.
Glasgow University Media Group (1985) *War and Peace News*, Milton Keynes, Open University Press.
Graber, D. (1984) *Processing the News, How People Tame the Information Tide*, New York, Longman Inc.
Hall, S. (1970) 'A World at One with Itself', *New Society*, 18 June.
Hall, S. (1977) 'Culture, the Media and the "Ideological Effect" ', in Curran, J., *et al.* (eds) *Mass Communication and Society*, London, Edward Arnold.
Hall, S. (1980) 'Encoding and Decoding', in Hall, S., *et al.*, *Culture, Media Language*, London, Hutchinson.
Hall, S. (1981) 'The Determination of News Photographs' in

Cohen, S., and Young, J. (eds) *The Manufacture of News*, London, Constable.

Hall, S., *et al.* (1976) 'The Unity of Current Affairs Television', *Working Papers in Cultural Studies* No. 9, University of Birmingham, CCCS.

Halloran, J., *et al.* (1970) *Demonstrations and Communications*, Harmondsworth, Penguin.

Harris, R. (1983) *Gotcha*, London, Faber and Faber.

Hartmann, P. (1975/6) 'Industrial Relations in the News Media', *Industrial Relations Journal*, Vol. 6, No. 4.

Hartmann, P., and Husband, C. (1972) 'Race and Mass Media', in McQuail, D. (ed.) *Sociology of Mass Communication*, Harmondsworth, Penguin.

Hetherington, A. (1985) *News, Newspapers and Television*, London, Macmillan.

Hodge, R., and Tripp, D. (1986) *Children and Television*, Cambridge, Polity Press.

Jones, N. (1986) *Strikes and the Media*, Oxford, Basil Blackwell.

Katz, E., and Lazarsfeld, P. (1955) *Personal Influence*, New York, Free Press.

Klapper, J. (1960) *The Effects of Mass Communications*, New York, Free Press.

Kuhn, T. (1962) *The Structure of Scientific Revolutions*, Chicago, University of Chicago Press.

Marcuse, H. (1955) *Eros and Civilisation*, Boston, Beacon Press.

Masterman, L. (1986) 'The Battle of Orgreave', in Masterman, L. (ed.) *Television Mythologies*, London, Comedia.

McQuail, D. (ed.) (1972) *Sociology of Mass Communication*, Harmondsworth, Penguin.

McQuail, D. (1977) 'The Influence and Effects of Mass Media', in Curran, J., *et al.* (eds) *Mass Communication and Society*, London, Edward Arnold.

Merton, R. (1946) *Mass Persuasion*, New York, Free Press.

Mills, C. Wright (1959) *The Power Elite*, Oxford, Oxford University Press.

Mills, C. Wright (1963) *Power, Politics and People*, Oxford, Oxford University Press.

Morley, D. (1980) *The Nationwide Audience*, BFI Television Monograph.

Morley, D. (1981) 'Industrial Conflict in the Mass Media', in

Cohen, S., and Young, J. (eds) *The Manufacture of News*, London, Constable.
Morley, D. (1981) 'The Nationwide Audience – a Critical Postscript', *Screen Education*, No. 39, pp. 3–14.
Morley, D. (1986), *Family Television: Cultural Power and Domestic Leisure*, London, Comedia.
Morrison, D. (1987) 'Policing Knowledge', *Media, Culture and Society*, Vol. 9, No. 3.
Murdock, G. (1973) 'Mass Media and the Construction of Meaning', in Armistead, N. (ed.) *Reconstructing Social Psychology*, Harmondsworth, Penguin.
Murdock, G. (1980) 'Misrepresenting Media Sociology: A Reply to Anderson and Sharrock', *Sociology*, Vol. 14, No. 3.
Murdock, G. (1981) 'Political Deviance – the Press Presentation of a Militant Mass Demonstration', in Cohen, S., and Young, J. (eds) *The Manufacture of News*, London, Constable.
Neale, S. (1977) 'Propaganda', *Screen*, Vol. 18, No. 3.
Observer (1984) 'Numbers Riddle at the Pits', 25 November.
Odeka, F. (1988) *Nigerian Enlightenment Campaigns*, University of Glasgow Ph.D. thesis.
O'Sullivan, T., Hartley, J., Saunders, D., and Fiske, J. (1983) *Key Concepts in Communication*, London, Methuen.
Phillipson, M., and Roche, M. (1971) Unpublished paper on phenomenological sociology, quoted in Taylor, I., Walton, P., and Young, J. (1973) *The New Criminology*, London, Routledge and Kegan Paul.
Philo, G., Beharrell, P., and Hewitt, J. (1977) 'Television News and the Control of Information', in Beharrell, P., and Philo, G., *Trade Unions and the Media*, London, Macmillan.
Philo, G., Hewitt, J., and Beharrell, P. (1980) Reply to Ian Connell, *Marxism Today*, October.
Porter, H. (1984) *Lies, Damned Lies and Some Exclusives*, London, Chatto and Windus.
Rogers, E., and Dearing, J. (1988) 'Agenda-Setting Research: Where has it been, where is it going?', *Communication Yearbook*.
Root, J. (1986) *Open the Box*, London, Comedia.
Schiff, S. (1985) 'What *Dynasty* says about America', *Vanity Fair*, Vol. 47, No. 12.
Schlesinger, P. (1978) *Putting Reality Together*, London, Constable.

Sparks, C. (1987) 'Striking Results?', *Media, Culture and Society*, Vol. 9, No. 3.
Summers, S. (1985) 'TV's Power Failure', *The Sunday Times*, 29 September.
Taylor, L., and Mullan, R. (1986) *Uninvited Guests*, London, Chatto and Windus.
Thompson, E.P. (1978) *The Poverty of Theory*, London, Merlin.
Tracey, M. (1986) 'Less than meets the Eye', *Listener*, 13 November.
Trenaman, J., and McQuail, D. (1961) *Television and the Political Image*, London, Methuen.
Voloshinov, V. (1973) *Marxism and the Philosophy of Language*, New York, Academic Press.
Williams, R. (1974) *Television, Technology and Cultural Form*, London, Fontana.
Wober, M., and Gunter, B. (1988) *Television and Social Control*, Aldershot, Avebury.
Wright, C. (1986) 'Mass Communications Rediscovered – its Past and Future in American Sociology', in Ball-Rokeach, S., and Cantor, M. (eds) *Media, Audience and Social Structure*, London, Sage.

Index